Everyday

Happiness

*21 Tiny Habits to Conquer Your
Stress, Experience Joy and Have a Content
Life.*

Dipaali Ghanshyam Patel
www.dipaali.life

DEDICATION

This book is dedicated to those who are
stresses and upset in their lives and seeking
simple but significant paths to experience
ecstasy in everyday life by implementing 21
tiny habits in everyday life.

Keep Learning, Keep Growing
and Keep Sharing
With Love,
Dipaali Ghanshyam Patel
www.dipaali.life

DOWNLOAD E-BOOK FOR FREE

Scan here to Download

Download the eBook "Affirm and Achieve" to manifest the desired results in every area of your life. There is a list of antidote and empowering affirmations to alter negative and critical self-talk. Practice them daily by using 9 secrets to manifest in your life.

Happy Practicing:
Visit to download E-Book
https://dipaali.life/download-free-ebooks/

INTRODUCTION

Knowledge is the power and Implementation of the knowledge can make us experience the real power. We now know the secrets of happiness and it's time to practice them in everyday life to be happy.

I read many books and attended workshops and seminars to learn to be happy, but I was not until I started choosing to be happy consciously.

One can choose to be happy consciously every day in all kinds of situations by setting a positive intention for the day. Outcome and Situation are not in your hands, but your interpretation is in your control. You will learn to tune your inner world by setting pure intention for the day. You will learn to take charge of your life by doing so.

Setting positive and pure intention brings attitude of gratitude. You will learn how to practice Gratitude to fuel your pure intention.

I was the workaholic. I end my day late night and my last minutes were with laptop and I start my day with laptop. Either I attend certain early morning seminars, or I conduct late night session. I either work at early morning or up to late night. My day starts and ends with gazettes. I didn't find to go out at the nature place to explore. I rarely got a chance to go out into the sunlight and as a result I was irritating and upset. I started experiencing joy with no reason when I choose to do "Digital Fasting" for few hours in a day.

I chose to take care of myself and accepted myself without judging. I join YOGA class for my physical and mental health. I realized that happiness doesn't need any fancy or big reasons. It is available in small and simple act in life.

My self-talk altered, and I started taking care of myself. I don't need reasons to be happy I choose to be happy. I Practice mindfulness and appreciate the beauty of life. I can see the bright side of challenging people and situations. I do practice finding the lessons to grow and let go which is not important to me.

I have taken charge of my life. It is in my hand to be happy. I can laugh louder now and that was the challenge for me for many years. I accept others as they are and I switched off the button of "Judgement" and "Criticism" from my inner world. I have started being kind to myself and have compassion for others. I am the happiest and I am being passed through the best time of my life. I am happy not because the absence of challenges but because I set my mind to be happy and content.

You will also learn by having 21 habits which have been shared in this book. Set your mind to be happy and all tools will give you wonderful result.

You will feel more joy and contentment in everyday life. You will feel power to deal difficult situations very easily. Your inner environment will not be disturbed even in non-favorable situations.

Practice all tools though your mind resist and you will create Happiness Mindset gradually.

Remember: Habits take time to develop in our lives, and everyday conscious choices help us to be happy.

Happiness is a choice, not a result.
Nothing will make you happy until you choose to be happy.

Ralph Marston

Table of content

CHAPTER – 1, SLEEP EARLY

One of the most famous Sanskrit quotes on the importance of going to bed early is

"Andhera hī raśmi ke bina vyāpāraḥ na kartavyaḥ,"

which translates to "Without the rays of the sun, no work can be done." This quote emphasizes the importance of waking up early in the morning, as the sun's rays help us stay active and productive throughout the day. By going to bed early, we can ensure that we wake up feeling refreshed and ready to tackle the day's tasks. So, if you want to be productive and successful, make sure to hit the bed early!

WHY SLEEP EARLY?

Getting enough sleep is essential for maintaining good health and well-being. While the amount of sleep required varies from person to person, it is generally recommended that adults aim for 7-9 hours of sleep per night. Going to bed early in the night can have several benefits for your physical and mental health.

- Our bodies are designed to follow a natural sleep-wake cycle, also known as circadian rhythm. Going to bed early and waking up early helps to align our sleep patterns with this natural cycle, making it easier for us to fall asleep and wake up feeling refreshed. This can improve the quality of our sleep and help us feel more alert and energized throughout the day.
- Going to bed early can also help to reduce stress and anxiety. When we are sleep-deprived, our bodies

produce more stress hormones which can make us feel irritable and anxious. Getting enough sleep can help to regulate these hormones and improve our mood.

- Getting enough sleep has been linked to a range of health benefits, including a reduced risk of heart disease, diabetes, and obesity. So, by going to bed early in the night, you are not only improving your sleep quality and mental health, but also reducing your risk of developing chronic health conditions.

In the case study, participants were asked to sleep early and get at least 7-8 hours of sleep per night for a period of 4 weeks. The study found that the participants who followed this routine reported feeling more refreshed and alert throughout the day. They also reported having more energy and improved productivity levels.

Additionally, the participants who slept early and got enough hours of sleep reported improved mood and reduced stress levels. They were able to handle daily stressors more effectively and had a more positive outlook on life.

The study found that getting enough sleep also improved the participants' physical health. They reported fewer instances of headaches, body aches, and illnesses.

HEALING TIME

The science behind this is that during deep sleep, the body produces human growth hormone (HGH), which is essential for growth and repair of tissues and muscles. Additionally, during deep sleep, the body produces cytokines, which are proteins that help fight infection, inflammation, and stress.

While the concept of specific healing occurring during a particular time, such as between 10 pm and 2 am, is somewhat simplified, it is based on the general understanding of the circadian rhythm and the sleep cycle. The body undergoes various crucial processes during sleep, and the timing of these processes is influenced by the body's internal clock, or circadian rhythm.

During the first part of the night, especially in the earlier sleep cycles, the body tends to focus on physical restoration and repair. Here are some key aspects of what happens when you sleep around 10 pm:

GROWTH HORMONE RELEASE

The release of growth hormone, which is essential for tissue repair, muscle growth, and overall development, tends to peak during the early stages of deep sleep. This peak often occurs in the first part of the night, especially during the first half of the sleep period.

CELLULAR REPAIR AND MAINTENANCE

During deep sleep, the body engages in cellular repair and maintenance activities. This includes the repair of damaged tissues, the removal of waste products from cells, and the regeneration of cells. These processes contribute to overall physical well-being.

MEMORY CONSOLIDATION

The first half of the night is also crucial for memory consolidation. The brain processes and consolidates information from the day, transferring memories from short-term to long-term storage. This supports learning and cognitive function.

Hormone Regulation

Sleep around 10 pm aligns with the body's natural circadian rhythm, influencing the release of hormones. Cortisol, which is associated with wakefulness and stress, typically decreases during the early part of the night, promoting a more restful sleep.

It's important to note that the sleep cycle is continuous, and these processes don't occur in isolation during a specific time frame. The sleep cycle consists of alternating stages of non-rapid eye movement (NREM) and rapid eye movement (REM) sleep, with each stage playing a unique role in the overall restoration of the body and mind.

While the hours before midnight are often considered beneficial for sleep quality, individual sleep needs vary. The most important factor is consistently obtaining the recommended 7-9 hours of sleep per night, regardless of the specific time you go to bed. Creating a regular sleep schedule, practicing good sleep hygiene, and prioritizing adequate sleep duration.

It's important to note that not getting enough deep sleep can lead to a variety of health problems, such as weakened immune system, poor cognitive function, and increased risk of chronic diseases. So, it's essential to prioritize getting enough restful sleep each night.

ANCIENT TIME

It is true that in ancient times, people's sleep patterns were different than what we see today. Without modern technology and electricity, people didn't have much to do after the sun went down, so they tended to go to bed early and wake up early with the sunrise. This was especially true in agricultural societies, where people had to wake up early to tend to their crops and animals.

In fact, many ancient cultures had specific customs and rituals around sleep. For example, the ancient Greeks believed that good sleep was essential for physical and mental health, and they practiced sleep hygiene techniques such as avoiding heavy meals and exercise before bed, and keeping their bedrooms cool and dark. The ancient Egyptians also had a deep respect for sleep and believed that dreams were a way to communicate with the gods.

HOW TO SLEEP EARLY?

Establishing a routine of low-stimulation activities before bedtime can help signal to your body that it's time to wind down and prepare for sleep. Here are some suggestions for low-stimulation activities to help you sleep early:

READING A BOOK

Choose a calming and non-stimulating book to read before bed. Avoid genres that may be overly exciting or suspenseful. opt for something that helps relax your mind.

LISTENING TO SOFT MUSIC OR PODCASTS

Soft, calming music or podcasts can be soothing and help create a peaceful atmosphere. Choose content that is gentle and doesn't evoke strong emotions or excitement.

TAKING A WARM BATH

A warm bath can help relax your muscles and create a sense of calm. Consider adding calming essential oils, such as lavender, to enhance the relaxation effect.

MINDFULNESS MEDITATION OR DEEP BREATHING

Engage in mindfulness meditation or deep breathing exercises to calm the mind and reduce stress. This can be a helpful practice to ease into a more relaxed state before bedtime.

STRETCHING OR GENTLE YOGA

Gentle stretching or yoga can release tension in the body and promote relaxation. Focus on poses that are gentle and don't require intense physical exertion.

DIMMING LIGHTS

Reduce exposure to bright lights, especially from screens, at least an hour before bedtime. Dim the lights in your environment to signal to your body that it's time to wind down.

JOURNALING

Write down your thoughts, feelings, or a to-do list for the next day. This can help clear your mind and prevent racing thoughts when you're trying to sleep.

HERBAL TEA

Enjoying a cup of caffeine-free herbal tea, such as chamomile or valerian root, can have calming effects and contribute to a sense of relaxation.

CREATING A COMFORTABLE SLEEP ENVIRONMENT

Ensure that your bedroom is conducive to sleep. Keep the room cool, dark, and quiet. Invest in a comfortable mattress and pillows to enhance your sleep quality.

AVOIDING STIMULANTS

Minimize the consumption of stimulants like caffeine or nicotine in the hours leading up to bedtime. These substances can interfere with your ability to fall asleep.

LIMITING SCREEN TIME

Reduce exposure to screens (phones, tablets, computers, and TVs) at least an hour before bedtime. The blue light emitted from screens can interfere with the production of the sleep hormone melatonin.

Establishing a consistent bedtime routine that incorporates these low-stimulation activities can help signal to your body that it's time to transition into sleep mode. Experiment with different activities to find what works best for you, and aim to create a calming and predictable pre-sleep routine.

There is an old proverb that says, "The early bird catches the worm." This saying emphasizes the benefits of waking up early and being proactive. Waking up early allows you to have more time to accomplish your goals and complete your tasks. It also provides a sense of calmness and allows you to start your day on the right foot. By waking up early, you can set the tone for the remainder of your day and be more productive. Additionally, studies have shown that waking up early can improve your mental health and increase your overall happiness. So, if you want to be successful and live a fulfilling life, it's important to make waking up early a habit.

WHAT DO DIFFERENT CULTURES SAY ABOUT GETTING UP EARLY?

Waking up early is a practice that has been valued in many cultures and religions throughout history. In fact, it is often considered a key to success and productivity. There are several valuable messages about the benefits of waking up early that can be found in various cultural and religious traditions.

In many cultures, waking up early is seen as a way to seize the day and make the most of the time available. This is often tied to the idea of hard work and discipline, as those who wake up early are thought to be more focused and productive. In addition, many cultures see early morning as a time for quiet reflection and meditation, which can set the tone for a peaceful and productive day.

In some religions, waking up early is seen as a way to connect with the divine. For example, in Islam, the first prayer of the day

(Fajr) is performed before sunrise, and it is considered a particularly important prayer. In Hinduism, waking up early is seen as a way to align oneself with the natural rhythms of the universe and to cultivate a sense of discipline and dedication.

In ancient Greek culture, waking up early was considered a virtue. The Greeks believed that waking up early was a sign of discipline, self-control, and hard work. The philosopher Aristotle, for example, believed that waking up early was essential for success and that it was the mark of a man who was serious about his life and work. The poet Hesiod also emphasized the importance of rising early in his work "Works and Days," stating that "the early bird catches the worm." This sentiment was echoed in other Greek literature as well, as the Greeks believed that waking up early allowed one to be more productive and efficient throughout the day. Overall, in

Greek culture, waking up early was seen as a key component of a virtuous and successful life.

ANCIENT INDIA

In ancient India, waking up early was considered a virtue and was highly valued. This practice was known as "Brahmamuhurta," which means "the time of Brahma," referring to the creator of the universe in Hinduism. According to ancient Indian scriptures, this time is considered to be the most auspicious time of the day for spiritual practices such as meditation, yoga, and prayer.

The period of Brahmamuhurta is approximately 1 hour and 36 minutes before sunrise. It is believed that during this time, the atmosphere is charged with positive energy, and the mind is fresh and clear.

Waking up in the Brahmamuhurat, which is the time between 4 a.m. and 6 a.m., can have several benefits for our physical, mental, and spiritual health.

- Waking up during this time can help regulate our circadian rhythm, which is our body's internal clock that regulates our sleep and wake cycles. This can lead to better quality sleep, increased energy levels, and improved overall mood.
- This time is considered to be very peaceful and serene, which can provide us with a great opportunity for meditation, introspection, and spiritual practice. It is believed that the energy and vibrations during this time are very pure and conducive to spiritual growth.
- Waking up early in the Brahmamuhurat can help us become more productive and efficient in our

daily lives. It gives us extra time to plan our day, exercise, and engage in other activities that we may not have time for later on.

Waking up in the Brahmamuhurat can have several physical, mental, and spiritual benefits. It is a great opportunity to start our day on a positive note and make the most out of our time.

EARLY RISERS

Many successful celebrities have attributed their success to waking up early and starting their day with a clear and focused mindset. One such celebrity is Dwayne "The Rock" Johnson, who is known for his early morning workouts and productivity. He often wakes up at 4am to start his day and has stated that this routine gives him a sense of control and sets the tone for the rest of his day.

Another celebrity who is a proponent of waking up early is Apple CEO Tim Cook. He reportedly wakes up at 4:30am every day to get a head start on his work. This routine has allowed him to be more productive and manage his time more efficiently.

There are many other successful celebrities who wake up early, including Oprah Winfrey, Michelle Obama, and Mark Wahlberg. While waking up early may not be the sole reason for their success, it has undoubtedly played a role in their ability to achieve their goals.

HOW TO WAKE UP EARLY?

If you're struggling to become a morning person, here are some tips to help you make waking up early a habit:

1. Create a consistent sleep schedule: Go to bed and wake up at the same

time every day, even on weekends. This can help regulate your body's internal clock and make it easier to wake up early.

2. Gradually adjust your wake-up time: Start by waking up 15 minutes earlier each day until you reach your desired wake-up time. This can help your body adjust to the change gradually.

3. Put your alarm clock across the room: This will force you to physically get out of bed to turn off the alarm, making it less tempting to hit snooze and go back to sleep.

4. Avoid electronic devices before bedtime: The blue light emitted by electronic devices can disrupt your sleep cycle, making it harder to wake up in the morning. Try reading a book or meditating before bed instead.

5. Have a motivating reason to wake up: Whether it's a morning workout or extra time to enjoy your morning coffee, having a motivating reason to wake up can make it easier to get out of bed.

Remember, it takes time and consistency to make waking up early a habit. Be patient with yourself and keep at it, and soon enough, waking up early will become second nature.

CHAPTER 3, EXERCISE REGULARLY

The Bhagavad Gita, revered Hindu scripture, impacts wisdom on various aspects of life, including in significance of physical activities. In chapter 6, Verse 17, Lord Krishna emphasizes the importance of moderation in all aspects of life, including exercise:

"Yukahara-viharasya yuktaceshtasya karmasu, yuktasvapnavabodhasya yoga bhavati duhkhaha."

This translates to "He who is temperate in his habits of eating, sleeping, working, and recreation can mitigate all material pains by practicing the yoga system."

Lord Krishna advocates for a balanced lifestyle that included appropriate engagement in physical activities. The Gita encourages individuals to maintain harmony in their daily routines, ensuring that physical endeavors are neither excessive nor neglected. Exercise, viewed as s form of self-discipline, is considered essential for overall well-being.

The Bhagavad Gita underscores the concept of "Karma Yoga," emphasizing the performance of one's duties and actions without attachment to the results. Engaging in physical activities is seen as a way to fulfill one's duty to maintain the health of the body, which is regarded as temple for the soul. By taking care of the physical self through exercise and healthy habits, individuals can contribute to their overall spiritual and mental well-being.

TYPES OF PHYSICAL ACTIVITIES

Regular exercise can have a significant impact on your mood and overall well-being. There are many different types of exercises you can do to improve your mood, including aerobic exercise, strength training, and yoga.

- Aerobic exercise, such as running, cycling, or swimming, can help increase the production of endorphins, which are chemicals in the brain that can improve mood and reduce stress levels. Aim for at least 30 minutes of moderate-intensity aerobic exercise, such as a brisk walk, on most days of the week.

- Strength training, such as weightlifting or bodyweight exercises, can also have a positive effect on mood. It can help increase self-confidence and improve body image, which can lead to a more positive outlook on life.

- Yoga and other mind-body exercises, such as tai chi or qigong, can be particularly effective in reducing stress and improving mood. These exercises combine physical movement with relaxation and meditation techniques, helping to promote a sense of calm and well-being.
- Walking: Walking is a great low-impact exercise that is easy to do every day. A brisk walk for 30 minutes can help to reduce stress, anxiety, and depression.

- Dancing: Dancing is a fun way to get moving and release endorphins. Put on your favorite music and dance around your room for a few minutes each day to help improve your mood.

Ultimately, the best type of exercise for improving mood is one that you enjoy and can stick to on a regular basis. Whether it's taking a dance class, going for a hike, or playing a game of basketball, find an activity that brings you joy and makes you feel good.

BENEFITS OF PHYSICAL EXERCISE

Exercising regularly has been shown to have a number of benefits for both physical and mental health. One of the keyways that exercise can help improve your mood and reduce anxiety is by releasing endorphins, which are the body's natural feel-good chemicals. These endorphins interact with receptors in your brain and trigger positive feelings in the body, similar to the way that morphine works to relieve pain.

In addition to the release of endorphins, exercise can also help to reduce levels of the stress hormone cortisol in the body, which can contribute to anxiety and negative mood states. By reducing cortisol levels, exercise can help to promote a more relaxed and positive state of mind.

Exercise can also help to improve overall physical health and well-being, which can in turn have a positive impact on mental health. By improving physical fitness, reducing the risk of chronic health conditions, and promoting better sleep and energy levels, exercise can help to create a more positive and balanced outlook on life.

Overall, there are many ways that exercising regularly can help to improve mood and reduce anxiety, making it an important part of a healthy lifestyle.

WHAT IF YOU DON'T DO ANY PHYSICAL ACTIVITIES?

If you don't engage in physical activities, you may be missing out on a variety of benefits that can improve your overall health and well-being.

Regular physical activity can help you maintain a healthy weight, reduce your risk of chronic diseases, improve your mood, and increase your energy levels. It's important to note that physical activity doesn't have to be intense or time-consuming - even small amounts of activity can make a big difference.

If you're not sure where to start, consider adding some low-impact activities to your daily routine, such as walking, yoga, or swimming. You can also try incorporating more movement into your day, such as taking the stairs instead of the elevator or parking further away from your destination to add in some extra steps. It's always a good idea to consult with your healthcare provider before starting a new exercise routine, especially if you have any underlying health conditions. Remember, any amount of physical activity is better than none at all, so try to find something you enjoy and make it a regular part of your routine.

Maintaining a non-active lifestyle, characterized by a lack of physical activity and prolonged periods of sedentary behavior, can have various negative effects on both physical and mental well-being. Here are some common side effects associated with a non-active lifestyle:

- Weight gain and obesity: Lack of physical activity contributes to weight gain and increases the risk of obesity. This, in turn, can lead to various health issues such as diabetes, cardiovascular diseases, and joint problems.

- Cardiovascular Issues: Sedentary behavior is a major risk factor for heart disease. A lack of physical activity can contribute to high blood pressure, elevated cholesterol levels, and poor circulation, increasing the likelihood of cardiovascular problems.
- Muscle weakness and atrophy: Without regular exercise, muscles can weaken and atrophy over time. This not only affects physical strength but also reduces the efficiency of everyday movements and activities.
- Bone health issues: Weight-bearing activities, such as walking or resistance training, are crucial for maintaining bone density. A sedentary lifestyle can lead to decreased bone mass and an increased risk of osteoporosis, especially as individuals age.

- Joint Problems: Lack of movement can contribute to stiffness and joint problems. Regular exercise helps to lubricate the joints and maintain their flexibility, reducing the risk of conditions like arthritis.
- Metabolic Disorders: Physical inactivity can negatively impact the body's metabolism, potentially leading to insulin resistance and an increased risk of type 2 diabetes.
- Mental health challenges: Sedentary behavior is linked to an increased risk of mental health issues, including depression and anxiety. Exercise is known to release endorphins, which can improve mood and reduce stress.
- Poor sleep quality: Regular physical activity is associated with better sleep quality. A sedentary lifestyle, on the other hand, can contribute to sleep disturbances and insomnia.

- Reduced cognitive function: Lack of physical activity has been linked to cognitive decline and an increased risk of neurodegenerative diseases such as Alzheimer's. Exercise is known to have positive effects on brain health and cognitive function.
- Lowered immune function: A sedentary lifestyle may compromise the immune system, making individuals more susceptible to infections and illnesses.

To mitigate these side effects, it's essential to regular physical activity into daily life, aiming for a combination of aerobic exercise, strength training, and flexibility exercises. Even small changes, such as taking short walks or incorporation standing breaks during prolonged periods of sitting, can contribute to better overall health.

CHAPTER 4, SET AN INTENTION FOR THE DAY

Setting an intention at the beginning of the day to practice happiness in day-to-day life is important for several reasons.

- It allows us to focus our minds on what is truly important to us, and to actively seek out moments of joy and positivity throughout the day. By making a conscious decision to prioritize our own happiness, we are more likely to notice and appreciate the good things in our lives, no matter how small they may be.

- Setting an intention for happiness can help us to cultivate a more positive outlook on life overall. When we actively seek out and create moments of joy and positivity, we train our brains to look for the good in every situation, even when things are difficult or challenging. This can have a significant impact on our overall well-being and happiness levels, as we learn to approach life with a more optimistic and resilient mindset.

- Setting an intention for happiness can help us to build stronger, more meaningful relationships with the people around us. When we prioritize our own happiness, we are better able to show up for others in a positive and supportive way, which in turn can help to strengthen our connections with them and foster a greater sense of community and belonging. Overall, setting an intention for happiness is a powerful tool for creating a more fulfilling and satisfying life.

TUNE YOUR BEING AT THE BEGINNING OF THE DAY

Setting an intention for the day is a powerful habit that can help you stay motivated throughout the day. It involves taking a few moments in the morning to reflect on what you want to achieve and how you want to feel during the day.

You can choose your being for the day. Set your positive and vibrant being for each task of the day. It helps you to boost your positive mood and offers you guaranteed favorable results. Just like you choose to tune your favorite radio station or channel for feel good, and by doing so you would be happy similarly if you decide your loving, calm, co-operative being for the day or with the specific person for the day, you will get magical outcomes for that day.

Setting "Being" means you are setting intention for the day and always remember you will get it what you ask for. We can choose to be happy, co-operative, loving, calm, composed. It's powerful way you can design your day as you desired at the beginning of the day and thus you can design your life.

PURE INTENTION AND HAPPINESS

The connection between pure and positive intentions and happiness in our lives is a strong one. When we approach life with good intentions, we are more likely to experience positive outcomes. This is because our intentions shape our thoughts, emotions, and behaviors, which in turn shape our experiences.

When we have pure and positive intentions, we are more likely to act in ways that align with those intentions. For example, if our intention is to be kind to others, we are more likely to behave in a kind and compassionate way towards others. This can lead to positive interactions and relationships, which can contribute to our overall sense of happiness and well-being.

On the other hand, if our intentions are negative or selfish, we are more likely to act in ways that are harmful to ourselves and others. This can lead to negative outcomes, such as strained relationships, feelings of guilt or regret, and a sense of disconnection from others. Let's understand through wonderful story of an old man "Anand"

Once Upon a time in a small village, there lived an old man named Anand Anand was known for his infectious smile and unwavering happiness despite leading a simple life. People in the village were curious about the secret to his joy, and one day a young man named Arjun decided to seek his guidance.

Arjun approached Anand and asked, "Old man, always seem so happy what's your secret?

Anand smiled warmly and invited Arjun to join him on a stroll through the village. As they walked, Anand began to share his story.

"Many years ago," Anand began, "I was just like everyone else, chasing after wealth and success. I believed that accumulating material possessions would bring me happiness. One day, I heard about a wise sage living in the mountains who was said to hold the key to true happiness. Determined to find the secret, i embarked on journey."

After days of arduous travel, Anand finally reached sages dwelling will stop the sage welcomed him and asked, "Why have you come, my son?"

On the end explained his quest for happiness and eagerly awaited the sages's answer. The sage, however, surprised him with simple question: "what is the intention behind your search for happiness?"

Anand paused, reflecting on his motives. He admitted that, deep down he sought happiness to prove his worth to others, to gain admiration and validation.

The sage smiled knowingly. "True happiness," he said, "comes not from that you acquire, but from the purity of your intentions. If your intention is selfless and pure, happiness will find its way into your heart.

Anand, humbled and enlightened, returned to the village with transformed perspective. He embraced a life of simplicity, kindness, and gratitude, focusing on the well-being of others with the house expecting anything in return.

As Anand shared this story with Arjun, he emphasized, "Young man, the key to happiness lies not in the pursuit of selfish desires, but in the purity of your intentions. When you do good without expecting rewards, when you genuinely wish well for others, happiness becomes a constant companion."

Arjun took these words to heart and inspired by Anand's story, decided to lead a life driven by pure intentions. Over time, he discovered that true happiness was informed in external achievements but in the joy of making a positive impact on the lives of those around him.

And so, the village gained another example of how the simple act of living with pure intentions could unlock the door to lasting happiness. Anand continued to be oh beacon of joy, teaching others that genuine happiness reflects the goodness we cultivate within ourselves.

PRAYER TO SET THE PURE INTENTION.

You can practice prayer to set an intention for the day. It helps you to boost your confidence and positive thinking. It motivates you to do good deeds in a day. Prayer is a fuel for soul. It nourishes your body and mind.

Dear Universe (or God, or any other higher power you believe in), I am grateful for this new day and the opportunities it brings. I ask for your guidance and support as I navigate through the challenges and blessings of this day. Please help me to stay positive, focused, and present, so that I may make the most of every moment and be a source of light and love to those around me. May my actions and thoughts be in alignment with my highest good and the highest good of all.

Dear Universe, offer me the opportunities to serve the humanity for the day. Give me that wisdom to decode the positive message of every adverse situation. Give me such power where I can understand the positive lessons from every non-favorable people or places.

Thank you for your love and blessings. Thank you for all wisdom and patience. Thank you for making me safe. Thank you for divine guidance. Amen (or any other closing that feels appropriate to you).

Thank you, Thank you, Thank you.

TIPS ON HOW TO SET AN INTENTION

- o   Start by visualizing your day. Take a few moments to close your eyes and visualize what you want your day to look and feel like. Imagine yourself accomplishing your tasks, interacting with people, and feeling positive and motivated throughout the day. Visualizing your day can help you set an intention for the day and create a positive mindset.

o Set an achievable goal for the day. Setting an achievable goal for the day can help you stay motivated and focused throughout the day. Choose a goal that is realistic and achievable, and make sure it aligns with your priorities. Write down your goal and keep it in a place where you can see it throughout the day, such as your phone or computer screen.

o Create a plan for the day. Creating a plan for the day can help you stay organized and focused throughout the day. Write down your tasks for the day and prioritize them based on their importance and urgency. Break down your tasks into smaller, manageable steps, and schedule them throughout the day. This can help you stay on track and avoid feeling overwhelmed.

o Practice mindfulness throughout the day. Mindfulness is the practice of being present and fully engaged in the moment. Practicing mindfulness throughout the day can help you stay focused and motivated. Take a few moments throughout the day to pause and check in with yourself. Take a deep breath, notice your surroundings, and focus on the present moment.

o Take breaks throughout the day. Taking breaks throughout the day can help you stay motivated and avoid burnout. Take a few minutes every hour to stretch, walk around, or do something you enjoy. This can help you recharge and stay motivated throughout the day.

o Celebrate your achievements at the end of the day. Celebrating your achievements at the end of the day can help you stay motivated and feel positive. Take a few moments to reflect on what you accomplished during the day and how it aligns with your intention for the day. Celebrate your achievements, no matter how small they may be.

Chapter 5, Start Your Day With Gratitude.

Gratitude is the master key of happiness.

The attitude of gratitude is the practice of acknowledging and appreciating the good things in one's life. This mindset has been linked to increased levels of happiness and overall well-being. When someone focuses on what they are thankful for, they are less likely to dwell on negative thoughts and emotions.

Research has shown that practicing gratitude can increase positive emotions, reduce stress and anxiety, and improve overall physical health. The act of expressing gratitude can also lead to stronger relationships and a sense of social connectedness.

By cultivating a grateful mindset, individuals can shift their focus from what they don't have to what they do have, leading to a greater sense of satisfaction and happiness.

It's not happiness that brings us gratitude. It's gratitude that brings us happiness.

Starting your day with gratitude is a powerful way to set a positive tone for the rest of your day. When we intentionally express gratitude for the things we have in our lives, we shift our focus from what we lack to what we have, creating a sense of abundance and contentment. In this way, gratitude is a practice of happiness, a way of cultivating joy and positivity in our lives.

But gratitude is more than just a feel-good emotion. There is a growing body of research that suggests that practicing gratitude has numerous benefits for our mental and physical health. For example, studies have found that people who regularly practice gratitude are more resilient in the face of stress, less likely to experience depression and anxiety, and have better relationships.

One reason for these benefits is that gratitude helps us to reframe our thoughts in a more positive way. When we express gratitude, we are focusing on the good things in our lives, which can help to counteract negative thinking patterns. This can be especially helpful for people who struggle with anxiety or depression, as negative thinking can be a major contributor to these conditions.

Gratitude also has a positive impact on our relationships with others. When we express gratitude for the people in our lives, we are acknowledging their contributions and showing appreciation for their support. This can help to strengthen our relationships and create a sense of connection and belonging.

Another benefit of gratitude is that it can improve our physical health. Studies have found that people who practice gratitude have lower levels of inflammation, which is linked to a range of chronic health conditions. Gratitude has also been shown to improve sleep quality, which is important for overall health and wellbeing.

HOW CAN YOU START YOUR DAY WITH GRATITUDE?

There are many ways to cultivate a practice of gratitude, but here are a few ideas to get you started:

1. Keep a gratitude journal: Each morning, write down three things you are grateful for. This can be anything from a good night's sleep to

a supportive friend to a beautiful sunrise.

2. Practice mindfulness: Take a few minutes each morning to sit in silence and focus on your breath. As thoughts arise, try to let them go and return your attention to your breath. This can help to create a sense of calm and centeredness, which can make it easier to feel grateful.

3. Express gratitude to others: Send a text or email to someone you appreciate, thanking them for something they have done for you. This can be a small gesture, but it can have a big impact on both you and the person you are thanking.

Starting your day with gratitude is a simple but powerful way to cultivate happiness and positivity in your life. By focusing on the good things in your life, you can create a sense of abundance and contentment that can have far-reaching benefits for your mental and physical health.

BENEFITS OF PRACTICING GRATITUDE

There have been numerous studies on the benefits of practicing gratitude, and many case studies have shown its effectiveness. One such case study involved a group of individuals who wrote down three things they were grateful for each day for 21 days.

After the 21 days, the participants reported feeling more optimistic and happier overall. They also reported fewer physical symptoms of illness and better quality of sleep.

In another study, participants were asked to write a letter expressing gratitude to someone who had positively impacted their life.

After writing the letter, participants reported feeling happier, more satisfied with their life, and more connected to the person they wrote the letter to. These benefits persisted for up to one month after the study ended.

Overall, these case studies demonstrate the power of practicing gratitude. By focusing on the positive aspects of life, individuals can improve their overall well-being and increase their happiness.

IDEAS TO PRACTICE GRATITUDE JOURNAL

A gratitude journal is a powerful tool to cultivate positivity and happiness in your life. Practicing gratitude daily can help you focus on the good things in your life and improve your overall sense of well-being. Here are some ideas for things you can write in your gratitude journal every day:

1.   Write down something good that happened to you today. It could

be something as simple as having a delicious cup of coffee or receiving a compliment from a friend.

2. Reflect on the people in your life who support and care for you. Write down the names of those who have made a positive impact on your life and why you are grateful for them.

3. Think about the opportunities you have in your life. Write down the things that you can do that bring you joy, whether it's traveling, reading, or spending time with loved ones.

4. Write about your personal strengths and accomplishments. Take time to recognize the things you have achieved and the qualities that make you unique.

5. Keep a gratitude journal and write down three things you are grateful for each day.

6. Say thank you to someone who has made a positive impact on your life.

7. Practice mindfulness and focus on the present moment.

8. Take time to appreciate the beauty of nature.

9. Express gratitude for your health and well-being.

10. Take a moment to appreciate your loved ones and the positive impact they have on your life.

11. Write a letter of gratitude to someone who has made a difference in your life.

12. Practice random acts of kindness and express gratitude for the opportunity to help others.

13. Express gratitude for your job or career and the opportunity to grow and learn.

14. Take time to appreciate the simple pleasures in life, such as a good cup of coffee or a beautiful sunset.

15. Practice self-care and express gratitude for your body and all it does for you.

16. Take a break from technology and appreciate the present moment.

17. Practice gratitude for the challenges and lessons learned in life.

18. Take a moment to appreciate your home and the comfort it provides.

19. Express gratitude for the food you eat and the nourishment it provides.

20. Practice gratitude for the opportunities and experiences life has provided.

21. Take time to appreciate your hobbies and the joy they bring to your life.

22. Take a moment to appreciate your pets and the love they bring to your life.

23. Practice gratitude for the diversity and uniqueness of the world around us.

24. Take time to appreciate the beauty of art and creativity.

25. Express gratitude for the ability to learn and grow.

26. Practice gratitude for the positive qualities you possess and the progress you have made in life.

27. Take a moment to appreciate the power of community and connection.

28. Express gratitude for the opportunity to make a positive impact on the world.

29. Express gratitude to your teachers and mentors who have supported you and guided you for your betterment

30. Express gratitude to your parents. Remember their unconditional love and support.

Remember, the key to a successful gratitude practice is consistency. By taking a few minutes each day to focus on the good in your life, you can cultivate a more positive mindset and increase your overall happiness.

Chapter 6, Practice

Mindfulness

We either think about the past or worry about the future. We never be in the present moment. It is natural for us to think about the future and reflect on the past, but if we spend too much time worrying about what may happen in the future or dwelling on what has already happened in the past, we may miss out on experiencing happiness in the present moment.

When we worry about the future, we are essentially anticipating negative outcomes that may never come to fruition. This can lead to feelings of anxiety, stress, and fear, which can prevent us from fully enjoying the present moment. Similarly, when we dwell on the past, we may feel regret, anger, or sadness, which can also prevent us from experiencing happiness in the present.

By focusing on the present moment, we can fully immerse ourselves in the experiences and opportunities that are available to us right now. This can help us to appreciate the people, places, and things around us, and find joy in the everyday moments of life.

It is important to learn from the past and plan for the future, it is equally important to stay present in the moment and enjoy the journey of life as life is in the present moment. By doing so, we can cultivate a sense of gratitude, positivity, and happiness that can enhance our overall well-being and quality of life.

Mindfulness is the practice of being present in the moment. It involves focusing on the present moment and paying attention to what is happening around you without judgment. You can be happier by being mindful. By practicing mindfulness, you can reduce stress, improve mental clarity, and increase your overall well-being.

SEVERAL WAYS TO PRACTICE MINDFULNESS

There are several ways to practice mindfulness. You can try any one or different ways time to time.

5 MINUTES PRACTICE

One of the ways where you need to set aside time each day to practice mindfulness. This can be as little as five minutes or as much as an hour. Anyone can start with 5 minute mindfulness. Spend 5 minutes at the beginning of the day or before bedtime. Do nothing during these 5 minutes and simply watch your thoughts and watch your breath. You can do it by closing your eyes or with open eyes. 5 minutes manfulness practice is like a 5-minute break to the mind, you can practice it several time in a day to recharge your mind and body. Make it a regular practice so that it becomes a habit.

MEDITATION

One way to practice mindfulness is through meditation. Meditation involves sitting quietly and focusing on your breath. When your mind wanders, simply bring your attention back to your breath. This helps to train your mind to stay present in the moment. You can be calmer and more centered by practicing meditation.

Mindfulness has been a part of Indian culture for centuries, with roots in Hinduism and Buddhism. The ancient Indian text, the Bhagavad Gita, describes mindfulness as the practice of steady control of the senses, mind, and intellect. One of the most famous examples of mindfulness in ancient India is that of the Buddha.

Siddhartha Gautama, the Buddha, practiced mindfulness meditation for six years before achieving enlightenment. He focused on breath awareness, body sensations, and mental states. Through this practice, he gained insight into the nature of suffering and the path to liberation.

MINDFUL EATING

Practice mindfulness is through mindful eating. Mindful eating is a practice that involves paying full attention to the experience of eating, both the food itself and the act of consuming it. It draws inspiration from mindfulness, a concept rooted in Buddhist teachings that emphasizes being fully present and engaged in the current moment. Mindful eating encourages individuals to cultivate awareness around their eating habits, including the taste, texture, and sensations associated with food, as well as the thoughts and emotions that arise during the eating process. It also involves eating slowly and savoring each bite. By doing this, you can become more aware of your body's hunger and fullness signals.

MINDFUL MOVEMENT

Mindful movement is another way to practice mindfulness. This can be any form of movement that involves being present in the moment, such as yoga, tai chi, or walking in nature. By paying attention to your body's movements and sensations, you can become more aware of your body and its needs.

Mindful movement doesn't require additional efforts to being in the present moment. You can just watch all your steps or body movement all the time. It's the best way being in the present moment.

Remember: The person is the happiest who practice being in the present moment.

Mindfulness is a practice that can be incorporated into many aspects of our lives, not just during meditation or yoga. It involves bringing our full attention to the present moment and being aware of our thoughts, feelings, and physical sensations without judgment. Here are some examples of when you can practice mindfulness:

1. During daily activities: You can practice mindfulness while doing everyday activities like washing dishes, taking a shower, or even brushing your teeth. Focus on the sensations and actions involved in the task and bring your attention back to the present moment if your mind starts to wander.

2. During a break: Take a few minutes to practice mindfulness during your workday. Find a quiet place where you won't be disturbed and focus on your breath or a sound. This can help you feel more relaxed and focused when you return to work.

3. While exercising: Exercise can be a great way to practice mindfulness as it requires focus and attention on the body's movements. Whether it's yoga, running, or lifting weights, try to stay present in the moment and pay attention to your body's sensations.

Remember: mindfulness is a practice that can be done anytime and anywhere. Start with small moments throughout your day and gradually build up to longer periods of practice.

WHY CAN'T WE GENERALLY PRACTICE MINDFULNESS?

Some people may struggle to practice mindfulness consistently. Here are ten reasons why people may resist or give up on mindfulness and meditation:

1. Lack of time: Many people feel that they don't have enough time to devote to mindfulness practice.
2. Difficulty sitting still: For some individuals, the act of sitting still and focusing on their breath can be challenging and uncomfortable.
3. Skepticism: Some people may be skeptical of the benefits of mindfulness and may not believe that it can have a significant impact on their lives.
4. Fear of emotions: Mindfulness can bring up uncomfortable emotions,

which some individuals may be hesitant to confront.

5. Impatience: Mindfulness requires patience and persistence, and some people may not see results right away, which can be discouraging.

6. Distractions: With so many distractions in our daily lives, it can be challenging to focus on the present moment.

7. Lack of guidance: Without proper guidance or instruction, it can be challenging to know how to practice mindfulness effectively.

8. Physical discomfort: Some individuals may experience physical discomfort while meditating, such as back pain or stiffness.

9. Lack of motivation: Without a strong motivation or reason for practicing mindfulness, it can be challenging to maintain a consistent practice.

10. Difficulty integrating into daily life: It can be challenging to integrate mindfulness into one's daily routine, particularly if it conflicts with other priorities or responsibilities.

Despite these challenges, it's important to remember that mindfulness is a skill that can be developed with practice and patience. By starting small and gradually building up a regular practice, anyone can experience the many benefits of mindfulness in their daily lives.

SIDE EFFECT OF NOT PRACTICING MINDFULNESS

When we fail to practice mindfulness in our daily lives, we can experience a range of negative side effects that can impact our physical and mental health.

A side effect of not practicing mindfulness is increased stress and anxiety. When we are not fully present in the moment, our minds tend to wander, and we may find ourselves worrying about the future or dwelling on the past. This can lead to feelings of anxiety and stress, which can have a negative impact on our overall well-being.

Another side effect of not practicing mindfulness is decreased productivity. When we are not fully present in the moment, we may find ourselves easily distracted and unable to focus on the task at hand. This can lead to decreased productivity and difficulty completing tasks efficiently.

TIPS TO PRACTICE MINDFULNESS.

In today's fast-paced world, it can be difficult to slow down and focus on the present moment. However, practicing mindfulness can be incredibly beneficial for our mental and physical health. Here are some tips to help you increase your focus while practicing mindfulness:

1. Find a quiet place: It's important to find a quiet place where you won't be interrupted. This could be a room in your house, a park, or anywhere else that feels peaceful.

2. Set a timer: Setting a timer for your mindfulness practice can help you stay focused. Start with 5-10 minutes and gradually increase the time as you become more comfortable with the practice.

3. Focus on your breath: One of the most basic mindfulness practices is to focus on your breath. Simply sit comfortably and focus your attention on your breath as it goes in and out.

4. Notice your thoughts: As you practice mindfulness, you'll likely

notice that your mind starts to wander. When this happens, simply notice the thought and gently bring your attention back to your breath.

5. Practice regularly: Like any skill, mindfulness takes practice. Try to practice mindfulness for a few minutes each day, and gradually increase the time as you become more comfortable with the practice.

By following these tips, you can increase your focus while practicing mindfulness and reap the many benefits that come with this practice.

MINDFULNESS MEDITATION SCRIPT FOR PRACTICING HAPPINESS IN DAY-TO-DAY LIFE

To begin, find a quiet space where you can sit comfortably without any distractions. Close your eyes and take a few deep breaths, letting go of any tension or stress in your body with each exhale.

Now, bring your attention to your breath, noticing the sensations of each inhale and exhale as they flow in and out of your body. If your mind wanders, simply gently guide it back to your breath, without judgment or criticism.

As you continue to focus on your breath, begin to cultivate a sense of gratitude for all the blessings in your life. Think about the people, things and experiences that bring you joy and happiness, and allow yourself to feel grateful for them.

Finally, imagine a warm, glowing light radiating from your heart center, filling your entire body with a sense of love and happiness. Allow this feeling to expand beyond your body, radiating outwards and touching the people and world around you.

Take a few more deep breaths and when you are ready, slowly open your eyes and bring your awareness back to the present moment. Remember that happiness is a state of mind that can be cultivated through regular practice, so make time for mindfulness meditation each day to experience greater joy and inner peace in your life.

CHAPTER 7, SPEND TIME IN NATURE.

Nature has a profound impact on our mental and physical well-being. Spending time in nature has been shown to reduce stress, boost mood, improve memory and concentration, and even lower blood pressure.

One way nature helps heal us is through its ability to reduce stress. When we are surrounded by the beauty of natural surroundings like a forest, beach, or park, our bodies naturally relax. The sound of waves crashing against the shore, the rustling of leaves in the wind, or the chirping of birds can all help calm our nervous system and reduce feelings of anxiety.

Nature also has a way of increasing our sense of awe and wonder, which can improve mood and increase feelings of happiness. For example, a stunning sunset or a majestic mountain range can be awe-inspiring and remind us of the beauty and power of the natural world.

NATURE PLACES AND HAPPINESS

Nature has always been a source of comfort and peace for humans. It provides us with a serene environment that is free from the hustle and bustle of city life. Studies have shown that spending time in nature, whether it's a park, forest, or beach, can help reduce stress and increase happiness in humans.

One reason for this is that nature has a calming effect on our minds. When we are surrounded by natural beauty, our minds are able to relax and let go of the stresses of everyday life. The sound of birds chirping, the rustle of leaves, and the sound of running water all have a soothing effect on our minds and bodies.

Another reason why nature is important for reducing stress and increasing happiness is that it allows us to disconnect from technology and the digital world. We are constantly bombarded with emails, notifications, and social media updates, and it can be overwhelming. Spending time in nature allows us to disconnect from these distractions and focus on the present moment.

Psychologically speaking, nature has been shown to have a positive effect on our mental health. Studies have found that spending time in nature can reduce symptoms of anxiety and depression. It can also improve our mood and increase our sense of well-being.

Nature provides a calming and peaceful environment that can help us relax and unwind from the stresses of everyday life. Here are some ways that spending time in nature can improve our mood and reduce stress. Nature is known to have a therapeutic effect on the mind and body. Walking or hiking in nature can help us clear our minds and reduce feelings of anxiety and depression. The fresh air and natural surroundings can help us feel more grounded and connected to the world around us.

Spending time in nature can help us disconnect from technology, which can be a significant source of stress for many people. By unplugging from our devices and immersing ourselves in nature, we can give our brains a much-needed break from the constant stimulation of screens.

Nature places can help us foster a sense of awe and wonder, which can be incredibly beneficial for our mental health. Being in nature can remind us of the beauty and complexity of the world around us, which can help us feel more grateful and appreciative of our lives.

Overall, spending time in nature is an excellent way to improve our mood and reduce stress. Whether it's going for a walk in the park, hiking in the mountains, or simply spending time in our own backyard, nature has the power to heal and rejuvenate us in countless ways.

LIFESTYLE OF CITIES AND COUNTRYSIDE

The lifestyle of people living in metro cities is quite different from those living in the countryside. People living in cities are often busy with their work and other activities while those living in the countryside tend to have a more relaxed lifestyle. One of the most important differences between the two lifestyles is the role of nature.

In the countryside, nature plays a very important role in people's lives. Agriculture is the main occupation in many rural areas, and people rely on the land and natural resources for their livelihood. People living in the countryside also tend to be more connected to nature, and they often spend time outdoors, enjoying the fresh air and natural beauty of their surroundings.

On the other hand, in metro cities, nature plays a slightly different role. While there are many parks and green spaces in cities, people often have to go out of their way to connect with nature. However, the importance of nature for city dwellers cannot be overstated. Being surrounded by concrete and steel can be stressful, and having access to green spaces can help people relax and unwind.

HOW TO CONNECT WITH NATURE WHILE LIVING IN THE CITY

Living in a metro city can make it feel like it's impossible to connect with nature, but there are still ways to incorporate nature into your daily life. One way to connect with nature is to bring it into your living space. Adding plants to your home can bring a sense of calmness and help purify the air. You can also create a small garden on your balcony or terrace if you have one.

Another way to connect with nature is to make time for outdoor activities. Take a walk-in a nearby park or nature reserve, go for a hike or a bike ride, or find a nearby lake or river and go kayaking or paddleboarding. Being in nature can help you reduce stress, increase creativity, and boost your mood.

You can also consider joining a local environmental organization. Many cities have groups that organize events such as tree planting, park cleanup, and environmental conservation projects. This can be a great opportunity to meet like-minded individuals and contribute to your community while enjoying the benefits of being in nature. Overall, living in a metro city doesn't have to mean disconnecting from nature. By incorporating plants into your home, making time for outdoor activities, and joining local environmental groups, you can still connect with nature and enjoy its many benefits.

One popular quote about the importance of nature for happiness is by John Muir, who said.

"In every walk with nature one receives far more than he seeks."

This quote highlights the idea that spending time in nature can bring us immense joy and fulfillment, even if we didn't necessarily set out to find it. There is something about being in natural surroundings that can soothe our souls, clear our minds, and remind us of the beauty and wonder of the world around us. Whether we're hiking through the mountains, lounging on the beach, or simply taking a stroll through a park, being in nature can help us find happiness and peace in our lives.

CHAPTER 8, EAT HEALTHY FOOD.

Healthy food refers to foods that provide the necessary nutrients to our body to maintain good health and function properly. These nutrients include carbohydrates, proteins, fats, vitamins, and minerals. Healthy foods are typically whole or minimally processed, meaning they are as close to their natural state as possible. Examples of healthy foods include fruits, vegetables, whole grains, lean proteins (tofu, beans, and legumes), nuts, and seeds. It is important to eat a variety of healthy foods to ensure that our bodies get all the nutrients they need to function properly. Additionally, healthy food choices can help reduce the risk of chronic diseases such as heart disease, diabetes, and obesity.

The phrase "we are what we eat" refers to the idea that our health and well-being are directly connected to the quality and quantity of the food we consume. This means that the food we eat has a direct impact on our physical, mental, and emotional health.

For example, if we consume a diet that is high in processed foods, sugar, and unhealthy fats, we are likely to experience negative health outcomes such as weight gain, inflammation, and chronic diseases. On the other hand, if we eat a diet that is high in fruits, vegetables, whole grains, and lean proteins, we are likely to experience positive health outcomes such as improved energy, better mood, and a reduced risk of chronic diseases.

In addition to the physical benefits of eating a healthy diet, there are also many emotional and mental benefits. Eating a diet that is rich in nutrients can help improve brain function, boost mood, and reduce stress and anxiety. Overall, the phrase "we are what we eat" serves as a reminder of the importance of making healthy food choices to support our overall health and well-being.

FOOD AND MENTAL HEALTH

Food is an essential part of our lives, providing the necessary nutrients to keep our bodies healthy. However, food also plays a crucial role in our mental health. According to the Shreemad Bhagvad Gita, the food we eat can impact our thoughts, actions, and overall well-being.

In chapter 17, verse 8 of the Shreemad Bhagvad Gita, Lord Krishna states that food can be classified into three categories - Sattvic, Rajasic, and Tamasic. Sattvic food is pure, nourishing, and promotes a peaceful state of mind. Rajasic food is spicy, bitter, and can lead to restlessness and hyperactivity. Tamasic food is stale, tasteless, and can cause lethargy and dullness.

When we consume Sattvic food, it nourishes not only our body but also our mind. It promotes a peaceful state of mind, clarity, and a sense of well-being. On the other hand, consuming Rajasic and Tamasic food can lead to negative emotions such as anger, confusion, and depression.

Moreover, in chapter 6, verse 16, Lord Krishna states that "Yukta-ahaara-viharasya yukta-chestasya karmasu, yukta-svapnavabodhasya yogo bhavati duhkha-ha." This verse emphasizes the importance of balance in our food, activities, and rest. Consuming a balanced diet and engaging in activities that promote both physical and mental well-being can lead to a happy and fulfilling life.

In addition, in chapter 17, verse 10, Lord Krishna states that "Utkrishta-yati jantu nityam sarva-kshetreshu, tamas-tu yati rajas-tamah prakriti-jair-gunaih." This verse highlights the importance of consuming high-quality food that is grown and prepared with care. Eating food that is contaminated or prepared with harmful additives can lead to negative consequences for our physical and mental health.

Furthermore, in chapter 6, verse 17, Lord Krishna states that "Yuktahara-viharasya yukta-chestasya karmasu, yukta-svapnavabodhasya yogo bhavati duhkha-ha." This verse emphasizes the importance of moderation in our food and activities. Consuming too much or too little food can lead to physical and mental health problems, and engaging in excessive or inadequate physical activity can have negative consequences as well.

The Shreemad Bhagvad Gita emphasizes the importance of consuming a balanced diet that promotes both physical and mental well-being. Eating Sattvic food can lead to a peaceful state of mind, while consuming Rajasic and Tamasic food can lead to negative emotions. Furthermore, it is important to consume high-quality food that is grown and prepared with care, and to engage in activities that promote balance and moderation. By following these principles, we can promote our mental health and lead a happy and fulfilling life.

HOW TO CHOOSE HEALTHY DIET?

Eating healthy is essential to maintaining a healthy lifestyle. Here are some tips and techniques to help you choose to eat healthy food in your everyday life:

1. Plan your meals: Planning your meals ahead of time can help you make healthier choices. Take some time at the beginning of the week to

plan out your meals and snacks. This will help you avoid making impulsive decisions when you're hungry and pressed for time.

2. Eat a variety of foods: Eating a variety of foods ensures that you get all the nutrients your body needs. Include fruits, vegetables, whole grains, lean proteins, and healthy fats in your diet.

3. Read labels: When you're grocery shopping, read labels carefully. Choose foods that are low in sodium, saturated fats, and added sugars.

4. Cook at home: Cooking at home gives you more control over the ingredients in your meals. You can choose healthier options and limit the amount of salt, sugar, and unhealthy fats in your food.

5. Practice portion control: It's important to practice portion control to avoid overeating. Use smaller

plates and bowls to help you eat smaller portions.

6. Stay hydrated: Drinking water throughout the day can help you stay hydrated and avoid overeating. Aim for at least eight glasses of water a day.

HEALTHY FOOD OPTIONS

Eating healthy food is one of the most important things you can do for your overall health and well-being. Fortunately, there are many delicious and nourishing foods that are both tasty and healthy. Here are some examples:

1. Berries - Berries are packed with antioxidants, vitamins, and fiber. They are also low in calories and can be eaten as a snack or added to smoothies, yogurt, or oatmeal.

2. Leafy Greens - Leafy greens like spinach, kale, and collard greens are loaded with vitamins and minerals. They are also a great source of fiber and can be eaten raw in salads or cooked in soups and stews.

3. Nuts and Seeds - Nuts and seeds are a great source of healthy fats, protein, and fiber. They can be eaten as a snack or added to salads, oatmeal, or smoothies.

4. Whole Grains - Whole grains like brown rice, quinoa, and whole wheat bread are rich in fiber, vitamins, and minerals. They are also a great source of energy and can be eaten as a side dish or used as a base for salads and bowls.

5. Avocado - Avocado is a great source of healthy fats, fiber, and vitamins. It can be eaten on its own or added to salads, sandwiches, and wraps.

6. **Fruits:**

- o Berries (blueberries, strawberries, raspberries)
- o Apples
- o Oranges
- o Bananas
- o Mangoes

7. **Vegetables:**
   - o Leafy greens (spinach, kale, Swiss chard)
   - o Broccoli
   - o Bell peppers
   - o Carrots
   - o Sweet potatoes

8. **Whole Grains:**
   - o Quinoa
   - o Brown rice
   - o Oats
   - o Barley
   - o Whole wheat products

9. **Proteins:**
   - o Tofu
   - o Pulses

10. **Nuts and Seeds:**

- o Almonds
- o Walnuts
- o Chia seeds
- o Flaxseeds
- o Pumpkin seeds

11. **Dairy or Dairy Alternatives:**
    - o Greek yogurt
    - o Cottage cheese
    - o Almond or coconut milk (unsweetened)

12. **Healthy Fats:**
    - o Avocado
    - o Olive oil
    - o Fatty fish (salmon, mackerel)
    - o Nuts and seeds

13. **Herbs and Spices:**
    - o Turmeric
    - o Ginger
    - o Garlic
    - o Cinnamon
    - o Basil

14. **Lean Proteins:**
    - o Skinless poultry

- o   Lean beef or pork
- o   Tofu
- o   Legumes

15. **Dairy or Dairy Alternatives:**
- o   Greek yogurt
- o   Cottage cheese
- o   Almond or coconut milk (unsweetened)

16. **Healthy Beverages:**
- o   Water
- o   Herbal teas
- o   Green tea

17. **Dark Chocolate (in moderation):**
- o   High-quality dark chocolate with at least 70% cocoa content can be a tasty treat in moderation.

Remember, a balanced and varied diet is key to getting a wide range of nutrients. Feel free to combine these foods in different ways to create delicious and nutritious meals. Additionally, adjusting flavors with herbs and spices can make your meals even more enjoyable without sacrificing health benefits.

Incorporating these healthy and nourishing foods into your diet doesn't have to be boring or tasteless. Experiment with different recipes and cooking methods to find what works best for you and your taste buds.

Human beings are inherently social creatures, and the need for company plays a significant role in shaping our positive mood and overall well-being. The importance of social connections is deeply embedded in our evolutionary history. Throughout evolution, humans have relied on social bonds for survival, cooperation, and protection. As a result, our brains are wired to seek social interactions, and being in the company of others triggers the release of neurotransmitters like oxytocin, often referred to as the "bonding hormone," which fosters feelings of connection and happiness.

Positive social interactions contribute to emotional regulation and stress reduction. Engaging in conversations, sharing experiences, and having emotional support from others can provide a buffer against life's challenges. The sense of belonging that comes from being part of a community or having close relationships is vital for mental health. Loneliness, on the other hand, has been linked to various negative health outcomes, including depression and anxiety. The social environment also influences our behavior and perspectives. Interacting with others exposes us to different viewpoints, cultures, and ideas, fostering personal growth and a broader understanding of the world. Sharing positive experiences, laughter, and joy with others can amplify the positive emotions we feel. Celebrating achievements, milestones, or simply enjoying the company of loved ones contributes significantly to a positive and fulfilling life.

Furthermore, social connections play a crucial role in providing a support system during challenging times. Whether facing personal hardships, work-related stress, or life transitions, having a network of friends, family, or a community to lean on can make a substantial difference. The emotional support and practical assistance offered by others can help navigate difficulties, reducing the impact of stressors on mental well-being.

IDENTIFY POSITIVE PEOPLE

Identifying positive and genuine people in our lives is an important skill that can help us build strong and meaningful relationships. Here are a few tips on how to identify such people:

1. They are supportive: Positive and genuine people are always willing to lend a helping hand and support others in their endeavors. They are happy to see others succeed and will do what they can to help make that happen.

2. They are good listeners: Good listeners are people who listen with their full attention and show empathy towards others. They are not judgmental and do not interrupt or dismiss others' feelings or opinions.

3. They are honest: Honest people are truthful and transparent in their communication with others. They do not hide their feelings or intentions and are upfront about their thoughts and beliefs.

4. They are non-judgmental: Positive and genuine people are accepting of others and do not judge them based on their appearance, background, or circumstances. They treat everyone with respect and kindness.

5. They have a positive outlook: People who have a positive outlook on life tend to be positive and genuine in their interactions with others. They

focus on the good in people and situations and are optimistic about the future.

There's a saying that goes, "You are the average of the five people you spend the most time with." And there's no denying the truth in that statement. The people we surround ourselves with have a significant impact on our lives, including our happiness and success.

HOW CAN WE ASSOCIATE WITH POSITIVE PEOPLE

So, how can we associate with positive and successful people to improve our own lives? Here are a few tips:

1. Identify the people you admire: Make a list of people in your life or in your industry who you admire and who embody the qualities you want

to emulate. This could be someone at work, a friend, or even someone you follow on social media.

2. Make an effort to connect: Once you've identified the people you want to associate with, make an effort to connect with them. Reach out and ask to meet for coffee or lunch. Attend events where you know they'll be in attendance.

3. Be genuine: When you do connect with these people, be genuine and authentic. Share your own experiences and struggles and listen to what they have to say. Don't try to impress them or be someone you're not.

4. Offer value: People are more likely to want to associate with you if you can offer them something of value. This could be your skills, your knowledge, or simply your friendship.

By associating with positive and successful people, you'll be inspired to become the best version of yourself. You'll learn from their experiences and insights, and you'll be more likely to achieve your own goals and aspirations.

HOW DO WE IDENTIFY NEGATIVE PEOPLE?

Dealing with negative people can be challenging, especially when they are affecting your peace of mind. The first step in identifying negative people is to pay attention to how they make you feel. Do you feel drained, unhappy, or stressed after spending time with them? If so, they may be a negative influence on your life.

Negative people tend to have a pessimistic outlook on life. They may complain frequently, blame others for their problems, and focus on the negative aspects of situations. They may also criticize others and engage in gossip.

Another way to identify negative people is to look at their behavior. They may be rude, dismissive, or disrespectful to others. They may also be self-centered and only concerned with their own needs and desires.

To protect your peace of mind, it may be necessary to limit your exposure to negative people. You can also try to reframe your thinking and focus on positive aspects of situations, rather than dwelling on the negative. Surrounding yourself with positive, supportive people can also help you maintain a positive outlook on life.

HOW TO AVOID TOXIC PEOPLE?

First you need to identify negative people. The first step in identifying such people is to pay attention to how they make you feel. Do you feel drained, unhappy, or stressed after spending time with them? If so, they may be a negative influence on your life.

Negative people tend to have a pessimistic outlook on life. They may complain frequently, blame others for their problems, and focus on the negative aspects of situations. They may also criticize others and engage in gossip.

Another way to identify negative people is to look at their behavior. They may be rude, dismissive, or disrespectful to others. They may also be self-centered and only concerned with their own needs and desires.

To protect your peace of mind, it may be necessary to limit your exposure to negative people. You can also try to reframe your thinking and focus on positive aspects of situations, rather than dwelling on the negative. Surrounding yourself with positive, supportive people can also help you maintain a positive outlook on life.

Avoiding toxic people is a crucial aspect of maintaining one's mental and emotional well-being. Toxic individuals can drain your energy, create negativity, and hinder personal growth. One effective way to navigate away from toxic people is by understanding the concept of setting healthy boundaries, akin to creating a protective shield around yourself. Just as a shield deflects harmful attacks, establishing clear boundaries helps safeguard your emotional space. Recognizing and articulating your limits prevents toxic individuals from encroaching on your peace of mind.

Metaphorically, consider toxic people as weeds in a garden. Weeds, if left unchecked, can overshadow and stunt the growth of healthy plants. Similarly, toxic individuals can overshadow the positive aspects of your life and impede personal growth. By regularly tending to your emotional garden, you can identify and remove toxic influences, allowing the healthy aspects of your life to flourish. This metaphor underscores the importance of continuous self-reflection and maintenance to ensure a thriving emotional landscape.

Another strategy involves developing a "toxicity radar," analogous to honing your senses to detect potential threats. Much like animals in the wild possess heightened instincts to identify danger, cultivating awareness allows you to recognize toxic traits in individuals. Pay attention to consistent patterns of negativity, manipulation, or disrespect. By trusting your instincts and avoiding individuals who exhibit toxic behaviors, you can proactively protect your mental and emotional well-being.

In the metaphorical journey of life, consider toxic people as heavy baggage that hinders progress. Just as travelers lighten their load to move swiftly and enjoy the journey, minimizing contact with toxic individuals frees you from unnecessary burdens. Embracing the philosophy of letting go reinforces the idea that prioritizing your mental health is paramount. Shedding the weight of toxic relationships allows you to move forward with greater ease, focusing on positive connections that contribute positively to your life.

TIPS TO AVOID TOXIC PEOPLE IN LIFE

- Set boundaries: Create clear boundaries for yourself and communicate them to the toxic person. This will help you protect your emotional space.
- Trust your instincts: If someone makes you feel uncomfortable or

uneasy, trust your instincts and avoid them.

- Stay positive: Surround yourself with positive people and maintain a positive outlook. This will help you attract positive energy and repel negative energy.
- Avoid gossip: Toxic people often thrive on gossip and negative talk. Refrain from participating in gossip and avoid people who engage in it.
- Practice self-care: Take care of yourself physically, emotionally, and mentally. This will help you maintain a strong sense of self and resist toxic influences.
- Focus on solutions, not problems: Toxic people often dwell on problems and negativity. Focus on finding solutions and positive outcomes instead.
- Choose your battles: Not every battle is worth fighting. Learn to let go of

things that are not important and avoid unnecessary conflict.
- Seek support: Surround yourself with supportive friends and family members who can provide emotional support and encouragement.
- Learn to say no: Toxic people often try to manipulate and control others. Learn to say no and stand up for yourself.
- Trust yourself: Believe in your own judgment and trust your instincts. You know what is best for you and your well-being.

POSITIVE PEOPLE VS. TOXIC PEOPLE

Positive people can significantly contribute to our happiness by fostering a supportive and uplifting environment. Their optimistic outlook, encouragement, and genuine care can have a profound impact on our overall well-being. Consider a story where a positive friend consistently provides encouragement during challenging times. This friend acts as a beacon of positivity, offering a listening ear, sharing words of wisdom, and celebrating successes. This unwavering support not only boosts morale but also creates a sense of belonging and shared joy.

Positive individuals often radiate energy that is infectious. Their enthusiasm can inspire others to adopt a more optimistic mindset, leading to a ripple effect of positivity. In a workplace scenario, for instance, a positive colleague who approaches challenges with a can-do attitude can motivate the entire team to tackle projects with resilience and creativity. The collective positivity enhances the work atmosphere, making it conducive to productivity and collaboration.

On the contrary, negative people can have detrimental effects on our lives. Imagine a scenario where a consistently pessimistic friend habitually focuses on the downsides of every situation. Their negative energy may become draining, sowing seeds of doubt and discontent. Over time, exposure to such negativity can impact mental health, leading to increased stress and decreased overall happiness.

Negativity can also breed a toxic atmosphere, stifling personal growth and hindering progress. In a professional setting, a persistently negative coworker may resist change, discourage innovation, and create a generally demoralizing work environment. The influence of negativity can permeate into various aspects of life, affecting relationships, decision-making, and overall life satisfaction.

From a logical standpoint, the impact of positive and negative individuals is often rooted in psychological principles. Positive interactions trigger the release of neurotransmitters like serotonin and dopamine, contributing to feelings of happiness and fulfillment. Conversely, prolonged exposure to negativity can elevate stress hormones such as cortisol, leading to heightened anxiety and a sense of dissatisfaction.

Let's understand through wonderful story.

Once upon a time in a small town, there were two friends, Emma and Olivia. Emma was known for her unwavering positivity, always seeing the silver lining in every cloud, while Olivia had a more skeptical and pessimistic approach to life. They both worked in the same company and often faced the challenges of a demanding work environment.

One day, their department was assigned a critical project with a tight deadline. The team was feeling the pressure, and the atmosphere was tense. Emma, with her positive outlook, decided to organize a team meeting to boost morale. She shared stories of past successes, highlighting the team's capabilities and emphasizing their potential to overcome challenges.

Emma's positivity became contagious. The team started to brainstorm more creatively, and individuals began supporting each other rather than dwelling on potential obstacles. As a result, the project progressed smoothly, and the deadline was met with a sense of accomplishment. The positive energy within the team not only enhanced the work environment but also strengthened team bonds.

In contrast, Olivia, being more inclined towards negativity, initially resisted the optimistic approach. However, witnessing the positive transformation in her colleagues and the overall success of the project, she began to appreciate the benefits of positivity. She realized that a positive mindset not only made the work more enjoyable but also significantly contributed to the team's effectiveness.

The story of Emma and Olivia illustrates the tangible benefits of positive people in a team or community setting. Emma's positive influence created an environment where challenges were seen as opportunities for growth, fostering collaboration and resilience. The team, inspired by Emma's optimism, not only met *the project's demands but also found joy in the process.*

This story reflects real-world scenarios where positive individuals can influence collective attitudes and contribute to achieving shared goals. Positivity often sparks motivation, resilience, and creativity, creating a ripple effect that transforms challenges into opportunities. Through Emma and Olivia's tale, we learn that the presence of positive people can uplift not only individuals but entire teams, leading to a more fulfilling and successful journey.

In essence, the company we keep plays a pivotal role in shaping our happiness. Positive individuals contribute to a nurturing and uplifting environment, fostering personal growth and well-being. Conversely, negative people can act as emotional drains, potentially impacting mental health and hindering overall life satisfaction. Recognizing and cultivating relationships with positive influences can, therefore, be a strategic and logical approach to enhancing happiness and maintaining a positive outlook on life.

CHAPTER 10, LAUGH

We don't need reasons to be happy, but to be upset. Laugh louder. Laugh at everything and be happy. Laughter is often referred to as the best medicine, and for good reason. Research has shown that laughter has numerous therapeutic benefits and can have a positive impact on both physical and mental health.

Laughter is a universal human experience that has been around for thousands of years. It is a physical reaction that occurs when we find something amusing or enjoyable. Laughter is often associated with happiness and joy, and it has been shown to have many positive effects on our physical and emotional well-being.

- Laughter releases endorphins, which are the body's natural feel-good chemicals. These endorphins promote an overall sense of well-being and can even temporarily relieve pain. Additionally, laughter can reduce stress and anxiety by decreasing the levels of stress hormones in the body.

- Furthermore, laughter has been demonstrated to improve immune function. A study conducted by Berk et al. (2008) found that laughter increases the production of antibodies and activates immune cells, which can help fight off infections and diseases.

- Laughter can also bring people together and foster social connections. When we laugh with others, we feel a sense of belonging and camaraderie, which can help reduce feelings of loneliness and isolation.

- Laughter is also a social behavior that helps to strengthen bonds between people. It can help to break the ice in social situations, ease tension, and build relationships. In fact, research has shown that people who laugh together are more likely to feel connected and to form lasting friendships.

- Laughing can boost your immune system. It increases the production of antibodies and activates immune cells, which can help to fight off infections and diseases. Furthermore, laughing can reduce stress hormones such as cortisol and adrenaline, which can weaken the immune system.

- Laughing can improve your mood and reduce anxiety and depression. When you laugh, your brain releases endorphins, which are natural feel-good chemicals that can improve your overall sense of well-being. Additionally, laughter can provide a temporary distraction from negative thoughts and emotions, giving you a fresh perspective on your problems.

- Laughing can improve your physical health. It can lower blood pressure, reduce muscle tension, and increase oxygen intake, which can improve circulation and promote relaxation. Additionally, laughing can provide a mild workout for the muscles in your face, stomach, and diaphragm.

- Studies have shown that people who maintain a positive outlook on life and have a happy disposition tend to live longer than those who are serious or negative. This is because being happy can help reduce stress and anxiety, boost the immune system, and promote a healthy lifestyle. On the other hand, people who are serious or negative tend to have higher levels of stress, which can lead to chronic health problems such as heart disease, diabetes, and depression. They also tend to engage in unhealthy behaviors such as smoking, excessive alcohol consumption, and poor diet, which can shorten their lifespan.

LAUGH LIKE A BABIES

Babies and children tend to laugh more frequently than adults. According to studies, babies laugh an average of 300 times a day, while children laugh an average of 150 times a day. This is because they are more easily amused and find joy in simple things like playing, singing, and dancing.

As we grow older, our sense of humor becomes more complex, and we tend to laugh less frequently. Adults think logically and logical thinking don't offer humor in our life. On average, adults laugh about 15 times a day or less than that. However, this can vary depending on personality, social environment, and personal circumstances.

So, how frequently should we be laughing as an adult? There is no set answer to this question, as it varies from person to person. However, it is important to make laughter a regular part of our lives. Laughing has numerous benefits, including reducing stress, improving mood, and boosting the immune system. Therefore, it is recommended that we find ways to incorporate humor and laughter into our daily lives to promote overall health and well-being.

Once upon a time, there was a man named Jack who was going through a rough patch in life. He was always stressed and had no time for laughter. One day, he met an old friend who invited him to a comedy show. Jack was hesitant at first, but he decided to give it a try.

At the show, Jack laughed so hard that he forgot all of his worries. He felt lighter and happier than he had in a long time. When he went home that night, he realized that his problems didn't seem so big anymore.

From that day on, Jack made a conscious effort to include laughter in his daily routine. He watched funny movies, spent time with friends who made him laugh, and even started cracking jokes himself. He found that laughter not only improved his mood, but it also strengthened his relationships and helped him cope with stress.

Over time, Jack's life improved significantly. He became more optimistic and started to see the good in his life. All of this was thanks to the power of laughter. So, if you're feeling down, try to find something that makes you laugh. You might be surprised at the positive impact it can have on your life.

FAKE IT TILL YOU MAKE IT.

"Fake it till you make it" is a common phrase that suggests that by pretending to be confident or happy, you can eventually become that way for real. One way to do this is through fake laughter. While it may seem silly, studies have shown that even fake laughter can have real benefits for our mood and overall well-being. When we laugh, our brains release endorphins, which are chemicals that make us feel good. So, even if we are laughing for no reason, our bodies still respond by making us feel happier and more relaxed.

There are many ways to laugh, and each person's laugh is unique to them. Some people have loud, boisterous laughs, while others have more subdued chuckles. We can also laugh in different situations, such as when we are watching a funny movie, telling a joke, or just spending time with friends. Some people even practice laughter yoga, where they intentionally laugh for the health benefits.

In conclusion, while fake laughter may seem strange, it can actually bring real joy and benefits to our lives. So, don't be afraid to let out a good laugh, whether it's real or fake, and enjoy the positive effects it can have on your mood and well-being.

LAUGHTER IS INFECTIOUS.

Yes, laughter is infectious! It is a well-known fact that laughter is contagious and can spread easily from one person to another. When we hear laughter, it triggers areas in our brain that are responsible for activating the release of feel-good chemicals such as dopamine, endorphins, and serotonin. This makes us more likely to join in and laugh along with the person who started it.

In fact, there have been several studies conducted to demonstrate the contagious nature of laughter. One study conducted by the University College London found that people are 30 times more likely to laugh when they are with others than when they are alone. Additionally, the study found that laughter is more contagious when it is genuine rather than forced.

Another interesting case study was conducted by Robert Provine, a neuroscientist and psychology professor at the University of Maryland. In his study, he observed people in natural settings and recorded their laughter. He found that people were more likely to laugh in social situations rather than when they were alone. Additionally, he found that laughter was contagious, with one person's laughter often leading to laughter in others.

Overall, laughter is a highly infectious and social behavior that has been observed across cultures and countries. It has been shown to have numerous physical and mental health benefits and can help to strengthen social bonds between individuals.

A day without laughter is a day wasted.

Charlie Chaplin

Smiling is infectious,
You catch it like the flu,
When someone smiled at me today,
I started smiling too.

I passed around the corner,
And someone saw my grin,

When he smiled, I realized,
I'd passed it on to him.

I thought about that smile,
Then realized its worth,
A single smile, just like mine,
Could travel round the earth.

So, if you feel a smile begin,
Don't leave it undetected,
Let's start an epidemic quick,
And get the world infected!

Pets have been a part of human life for thousands of years, and it's no secret that many of us love them dearly. But why do we feel such a strong connection to these furry (or feathered, or scaly) creatures?

One reason may be that pets provide companionship and unconditional love. They are always there for us, no matter what, and they are often very affectionate. This can be especially important for people who live alone or who have limited social interactions.

Additionally, pets can provide a sense of purpose and responsibility. Taking care of a pet requires time, effort, and attention, and this can give us a sense of accomplishment and fulfillment. Pets can also help us to stay active and healthy, by encouraging us to exercise and spend time outdoors.

many people simply enjoy the joy and happiness that pets bring into their lives. Whether it's watching a playful kitten chase a toy or snuggling up with a loyal dog on the couch, pets have a way of making us feel happy and content.

SOME POPULAR PETS

Some popular pets include dogs, cats, birds, fish, and small mammals like hamsters, guinea pigs, and rabbits.

Dogs are known for their loyalty and companionship and come in many breeds and sizes. They require regular exercise and training but can be a wonderful addition to an active household. Cats are independent and low-maintenance and make great indoor companions. They are known for their playful and curious nature, and can form strong bonds with their owners.

Birds are colorful and entertaining pets that can provide hours of enjoyment with their singing and playful behavior. They require specialized care, such as a spacious cage, a balanced diet, and regular interaction. Fish are calming and peaceful pets that can be kept in aquariums and require minimal care.

Small mammals like hamsters, guinea pigs, and rabbits are popular pets for children and adults alike. They are low-maintenance and can be kept indoors, but require a clean and spacious living environment, a balanced diet, and regular attention.

PETS & HUMAN'S HAPPINESS

The connection between mental health and pets is a fascinating subject. Studies have shown that pets can have a positive impact on a person's mental health and emotional well-being. In this case study, we will explore the story of a woman named Sarah, who has struggled with depression and anxiety for many years, and how her pets have helped her cope.

Sarah had been diagnosed with depression and anxiety in her early twenties. She had tried various treatments, including therapy and medication, but nothing seemed to help. One day, she decided to adopt a dog from a local animal shelter. She named him Max. Max quickly became her constant companion, always by her side, giving her unconditional love and support.

Sarah found that taking care of Max gave her a sense of purpose and responsibility. She also found that the act of petting him and playing with him helped to reduce her stress and anxiety. Max's presence helped her to feel less alone and isolated, and she found that she was able to open up more to others.

A few years later, Sarah adopted a cat named Luna. Luna was a rescue cat, and Sarah could tell that she had been through a lot in her life. Sarah found that caring for Luna helped her to feel more compassionate and caring towards herself. She also found that the act of snuggling with Luna helped her to feel more relaxed and calmer.

In conclusion, Sarah's pets, Max and Luna, have had a significant positive impact on her mental health. They have provided her with companionship, love, and support when she needed it most.

Pets can be a great source of comfort and joy for those struggling with mental health issues.

Pets are much more than just cute and cuddly companions. They can have a significant impact on our overall happiness and well-being. Here are some of the most important benefits of having pets:

1. Reduced stress and anxiety: Studies have shown that spending time with pets can help reduce stress and anxiety levels. Petting a dog or cat can lower blood pressure and release feel-good hormones such as oxytocin and serotonin.

2. Increased physical activity: Owning a pet can also encourage physical activity and exercise.

Walking a dog or playing with a cat can help improve cardiovascular health and reduce the risk of obesity.

3. Improved social connections: Pets can also help improve our social connections and reduce feelings of loneliness. Walking a dog or taking them to a dog park can lead to interactions with other pet owners, while simply having a pet around can provide a sense of companionship.

4. Emotional support: Pets can provide emotional support and comfort during difficult times. They can be a source of unconditional love and can help alleviate feelings of depression and anxiety.

There is a well-known quote that says "A good book is like a good friend. It will stay with you for the rest of your life." This quote highlights the idea that just like a loyal friend, a good book can be relied upon to provide comfort, wisdom, and entertainment whenever we need it. Books can become our companions in times of loneliness, our teachers in times of uncertainty, and our escape from the stresses of everyday life. They can challenge our perspectives, broaden our horizons, and inspire us to become better versions of ourselves. So, if you're ever feeling lost or alone, just remember that a good book is always there to be your faithful friend.

The belief that reading books can heal your mind is rooted in the idea that literature has the power to transport us into different worlds, perspectives, and experiences. When we read, we engage our imaginations and our emotions, and we become more empathetic and open-minded individuals.

Studies have shown that reading can also have concrete benefits for our mental health. For example, it can reduce stress and anxiety, improve our ability to focus and concentrate, and even slow down the progression of neurodegenerative diseases such as Alzheimer's.

Reading can be a form of self-care and a way to take a break from the stressors of daily life. It can help us to unwind, relax, and recharge, allowing us to return to our responsibilities with a clearer and more centered mindset.

Reading books can help improve one's vocabulary, language skills, and cognitive abilities. It also helps reduce stress and improve focus and concentration. Reading books on different topics can broaden one's knowledge and perspective on various subjects. Reading books can also improve one's memory and critical thinking skills.

As per a survey conducted by Pew Research Center, the average number of books an American read in a year is 12. However, this number varies greatly based on individual preferences and habits. It is important to make reading a part of one's daily routine as it can have a positive impact on overall well-being.

Remember: Readers are the leaders. The one who reads can leads the life happily in every circumstances.

CHAPTER 13, LEARN NEW THINGS

The idea that learners can lead is rooted in the belief that knowledge and leadership are not exclusively possessed by a select few individuals. Learning is a lifelong process that empowers people to continually acquire new knowledge and skills, and this process can be facilitated by anyone regardless of their position or title. When learners take initiative and actively seek out new information, they can become experts in their fields and lead by example.

Moreover, learners can lead by sharing their knowledge with others and inspiring them to become lifelong learners themselves. When learners become teachers and mentors, they create a culture of learning that benefits not only themselves but their communities as well. By sharing their knowledge and leading by example, learners can foster a collaborative and inclusive environment that encourages growth and development.

ATTITUDE OF LEARNING NEW THINGS

Learning new things is essential for personal growth, happiness, and success. It expands our knowledge, enhances our skills, and broadens our perspectives. Here are some new things you can learn to achieve happiness and success:

1. Learn a new language: Learning a new language opens up new opportunities for personal and professional growth. It expands your communication skills,

enhances your problem-solving abilities, and exposes you to diverse cultures and backgrounds.

2. Develop a new skill: Developing a new skill, such as cooking, coding, or playing a musical instrument, can boost your confidence, improve your creativity, and provide a sense of accomplishment.

3. Travel to new places: Travelling to new places exposes you to different cultures, customs, and ways of life. It broadens your horizons, enhances your understanding of the world, and helps you develop an appreciation for diversity.

4. Read more books: Reading is a great way to gain knowledge,

improve your vocabulary, and reduce stress. It also stimulates your imagination and enhances your critical thinking skills.

5. Learn a new hobby: Learning a new hobby, such as painting, gardening, or photography, can provide a sense of fulfillment and relaxation. It also helps you develop new skills and explore new interests.

HAPPINESS AND LEARNING NEW THINGS

Having a positive attitude towards learning difficult skills can actually help improve our mood. When we approach a challenging task with a growth mindset, we believe that we can improve and develop our abilities through hard work and dedication. This type of attitude can help us stay motivated and persevere through obstacles, which in turn can boost our confidence and sense of accomplishment.

Furthermore, learning a new skill can be a great way to combat feelings of boredom or stagnation. When we challenge ourselves and engage in new experiences, it can help us feel more energized, fulfilled, and purposeful. This can lead to increased feelings of happiness and satisfaction with life.

LEARNING NEW THINGS VS. NOT READY TO LEARN NEW THINGS

individuals to broaden their knowledge, expand their skillset and improve their overall quality of life. Not learning new things, on the other hand, can lead to stagnation and a sense of complacency.

One significant difference between not learning new things and learning new things is the impact it has on an individual's mental and emotional well-being. Learning new things can boost self-confidence, self-esteem, and provide a sense of accomplishment. On the other hand, not learning new things can lead to boredom, frustration, and even depression.

Another difference between not learning new things and learning new things is the impact it can have on one's professional life. Learning new skills and knowledge can make an individual more marketable and competitive in the job market. It can also lead to career advancement opportunities and increased earning potential. On the other hand, not learning new things can lead to a lack of growth and potential career stagnation.

Actually, learning new things is an essential aspect of personal and professional development. It can lead to increased mental and emotional well-being, improved career opportunities, and overall personal growth. Not learning new things can lead to stagnation and a lack of growth, which can have a negative impact on an individual's life.

IMPORTANCE OF CONSISTENCE LEARNINGS

Consistent learning is crucial for human beings for a variety of reasons.

- Learning helps to keep our minds active and engaged. It has been proven that consistent learning can help to improve cognitive functions and even slow down the aging process. By learning new things regularly, we can keep our brains sharp and alert.
- Consistent learning helps us to adapt to changes and challenges in our lives. In today's fast-paced world, it is important to be able to learn new skills and technologies quickly in order to stay competitive and succeed in our careers. Learning also helps us to become more resilient and better equipped to handle difficult situations.
- Learning can bring a sense of fulfillment and satisfaction to our

lives. Whether we are learning a new language, taking up a new hobby, or exploring a new subject, the process of learning can be both enjoyable and rewarding. Learning can also help us to connect with others who share our interests and passions.

REAL LIFE LEADERS

There are many real-life examples of individuals who are dedicated to lifelong learning and personal growth.

- Elon Musk, the founder of SpaceX, Tesla, and several other successful companies. Despite already achieving great success, Musk is known for being a voracious reader and constantly seeking out new knowledge and skills. He has even been known to work up to 100 hours a week and sleep at his office to further his goals.

- Oprah Winfrey, who is a media mogul, actress, and philanthropist. Winfrey has spoken publicly about her commitment to self-improvement and growth, both personally and professionally. She has shared that she regularly reads and attends seminars to expand her knowledge and constantly strives to become a better version of herself.

- Jack Ma, the founder of Alibaba Group, is also a well-known example of someone who values lifelong learning and growth.

Despite facing numerous setbacks and rejections in his early career, Ma persevered and continued to learn from his experiences. He has since become a successful entrepreneur and a prominent advocate for education and personal development.

These individuals demonstrate that a commitment to ongoing learning and growth can lead to great success and personal fulfillment.

Overall, having a positive attitude towards learning new and difficult skills can help us improve our mood by increasing our motivation, confidence, and sense of purpose. So the next time you're faced with a challenging task, try approaching it with a growth mindset and see how it affects your mood!

Chapter 14, Music

Music has been known to have a powerful healing effect on the mind, body, and soul. As the famous musician Bob Marley once said, "One good thing about music, when it hits you, you feel no pain." This quote highlights the transformative power of music, which can help us forget our troubles, ease our pain, and lift our spirits. Music has been shown to reduce stress and anxiety, boost our mood, and even help us recover from physical illnesses. Whether it's through singing, playing an instrument, or simply listening to our favorite songs, music has the power to heal us in ways that few other things can.

MUSIC THERAPY IN ANCIENT INDIA

Ancient Indian history of music dates to the Vedic era, which is around 1500 BCE. During this time, music was used for religious ceremonies, and it was believed that the chanting of mantras and hymns could bring inner peace and alleviate stress. The Indian classical music system, also known as Hindustani music, has evolved over the centuries and is considered one of the oldest and most complex systems of music in the world.

Music therapy has been an integral part of Indian culture for centuries. Indian classical music, with its complex melodies and rhythms, has been used to treat a variety of mental and physical ailments. It is believed that the vibrations and frequencies of music can have a profound effect on the body and mind.

In Ayurveda, the traditional Indian system of medicine, music is considered a powerful tool for healing. It is believed that music can balance the three doshas (Vata, Pitta, Kapha) and bring the body and mind into a state of harmony. Music therapy is also used to treat a variety of mental health conditions such as depression, anxiety, and stress.

Music has played a significant role in ancient Indian culture, and it continues to be an integral part of Indian life today. The therapeutic benefits of music have been recognized for centuries, and Indian classical music remains a popular form of music therapy to this day.

MUSIC FOR MENTAL HEALTH

Music has been known to have a positive impact on mental health, and there are several types of music that can help promote it. One type of music that is particularly effective for reducing stress and anxiety is classical music. The soothing melodies and rhythms of classical music can help to calm the mind and promote relaxation.

Another type of music that can be beneficial for mental health is nature sounds such as rain, ocean waves, or birds chirping. These sounds can help to create a peaceful and calming environment, which can be helpful for reducing stress and promoting relaxation.

For those who prefer more upbeat music, listening to songs with positive lyrics and a fast tempo can be helpful for boosting mood and energy levels. This can include genres such as pop, rock, and electronic dance music (EDM).

Ultimately, the type of music that is best for mental health will vary from person to person. It is important to listen to music that resonates with you and brings you joy and comfort.

One study published in the Journal of Advanced Nursing found that listening to music can help reduce stress and anxiety levels in patients undergoing medical procedures. The study showed that patients who listened to music before and after surgery had lower levels of anxiety and reported feeling calmer and more relaxed.

Another study published in the Journal of Music Therapy found that music therapy can be an effective form of treatment for individuals with depression. The study showed that participants who received music therapy had lower levels of depression and anxiety compared to those who did not receive music therapy.

Research has shown that music can also have physical benefits such as reducing pain and improving immune function. A study published in the Journal of Pain and Symptom Management found that patients with chronic pain who listened to music for just one hour a day reported a significant reduction in pain compared to those who did not listen to music.

Overall, there is a growing body of research that supports the therapeutic benefits of music. Whether it's listening to music to reduce stress and anxiety, or using music therapy as a treatment for depression, music has the power to heal both the mind and body.

One famous quote about music as therapy comes from American musician Billy Joel: "I think music in itself is healing. It's an explosive expression of humanity. It's something we are all touched by. No matter what culture we're from, everyone loves music." This quote highlights the universal power of music to connect people across cultures and backgrounds, and to provide a healing outlet for emotions and experiences. Many studies have shown that music therapy can be effective in reducing stress, managing pain, and improving overall wellbeing. So whether you're listening to your favorite song to boost your mood or working with a trained music therapist, there's no denying the therapeutic benefits of music.

CHAPTER 15, DANCE

Dance is a form of expression through movement of the body, often accompanied by music or rhythm. It is a way to communicate emotions, ideas, or stories through physical gestures and sequences. Dance can be found in many cultures and traditions around the world, and can take on many different styles and forms, from ballet to hip-hop, from traditional folk dances to contemporary dance performances. Dance can be a form of entertainment, a means of exercise, a social activity, or a professional career. It allows individuals to express themselves in a unique and creative way, while also connecting with others through a shared experience.

Dancing is a universal expression of joy and celebration that transcends language barriers and cultural differences. It is a way for people to express themselves and connect with others in a fun and playful way. Even if someone doesn't know how to dance, they can still enjoy moving their body to the rhythm of the music and letting go of their inhibitions. Dancing can also be a great form of exercise that helps to improve cardiovascular health, flexibility, and coordination. So, even if someone doesn't know how to dance, they can still reap the many benefits of this enjoyable and healthy activity.

DANCE AND HAPPINESS

Dancing is not only a form of exercise, but it also plays a significant role in contributing to happiness in human life. When we dance, our bodies produce endorphins, which are natural chemicals that make us feel good. This is why dancing is often associated with feelings of joy and happiness. Additionally, dancing allows us to express ourselves in a unique way, which can help to boost our self-confidence and self-esteem.

Moreover, dancing provides an opportunity for social connection and interaction. Whether it's taking a dance class, attending a social event, or simply dancing with friends, it can help us to form bonds and create meaningful relationships. This sense of community can lead to increased feelings of belonging and happiness.

Dancing can also serve as a form of stress relief. When we dance, we can let go of our worries and focus on the present moment. This can help to reduce anxiety and promote relaxation, leading to an overall sense of well-being.

Dancing is a fun and effective way to promote happiness in human life. It provides physical and emotional benefits, fosters social connections, and can serve as a form of stress relief. So next time you're feeling down, put on some music and dance your cares away!

DANCE & MENTAL HEALTH

Dance can be suggested as therapy for mental health for a variety of reasons. Firstly, dancing can be a form of physical exercise, which has been shown to have a positive impact on mental health. Exercise can release endorphins, which are the body's natural feel-good chemicals, and can help reduce symptoms of anxiety and depression.

Dance can be a creative outlet, allowing individuals to express themselves in a non-verbal way. This can be particularly helpful for those who find it difficult to articulate their thoughts and emotions through words. Dancing can also provide a sense of accomplishment and boost self-esteem, as individuals learn new movements and become more comfortable in their own bodies.

It dance can be a social activity, providing opportunities for individuals to connect with others and form supportive relationships. This can be especially important for those who are struggling with feelings of isolation or loneliness. Overall, dance therapy can be a valuable tool for improving mental health and well-being.

Dancing or any physical movement can be incredibly beneficial for overall well-being. There are numerous benefits to engaging in physical activity, such as improving cardiovascular health, strengthening muscles and bones, and reducing the risk of chronic diseases. Additionally, dancing specifically has been shown to improve balance and coordination, boost cognitive function, and reduce stress levels.

One of the main benefits of dancing is the cardiovascular workout it provides. Dancing gets your heart rate up and can improve your endurance, helping to strengthen your heart and lungs. This can lead to a reduced risk of heart disease, stroke, and other cardiovascular conditions.

Dancing also helps to strengthen muscles and bones. As you move your body through different dance moves, you engage a variety of muscles and bones, which can help to increase strength and improve overall physical function.

Beyond the physical benefits, dancing has been shown to improve cognitive function as well. Research has found that dancing can help to improve memory, attention, and reaction time, as well as reduce the risk of developing dementia.

Dancing can be a great way to reduce stress levels. When you dance, you release endorphins, which are the body's natural "feel-good" chemicals. This can help to reduce feelings of anxiety and depression, and improve overall mood.

Dancing or any physical movement is highly advisable for overall well-being. It can improve cardiovascular health, strengthen muscles and bones, boost cognitive function, and reduce stress levels. So put on your favorite tunes and get moving!

In conclusion, dancing offers numerous benefits, ranging from improved cardiovascular health and balance to boosted mood and mental health. It is a fun and enjoyable way to stay active and healthy, regardless of age or fitness level.

CHAPTER 16, WATCH COMEDY MOVIE

People watch movies for various reasons. For some, it is a form of entertainment and an escape from reality. Movies can take us to places we have never been and introduce us to characters we can relate to or admire. They can also provide us with a sense of nostalgia, reminding us of past experiences or feelings. For others, watching movies can be a form of education or a way to learn about different cultures, history, or social issues. Movies can also be used as a means of relaxation or to relieve stress. Whatever the reason, movies have the ability to connect us with others and evoke emotions that can stay with us long after the credits have rolled.

COMEDY MOVIE AS THERAPY

Comedy movies have been known to be therapeutic for individuals as they can help alleviate stress, anxiety, and depression. Therapists often recommend their patients to watch comedy movies as a form of therapy because laughter has been shown to have numerous benefits on the mind and body.

When we laugh, our brain releases endorphins, which are chemicals that make us feel good. Endorphins can help reduce pain, boost our immune system, and promote overall well-being. Additionally, laughing can help reduce stress hormones such as cortisol and adrenaline, which can have negative effects on our body if they are chronically elevated.

Comedy movies can also provide a temporary escape from reality, giving individuals a chance to forget about their problems and just enjoy the moment. This can be especially helpful for people who are experiencing high levels of stress or anxiety.

When we watch a comedy movie or show, our brain releases endorphins, which are also known as "feel-good" chemicals. These endorphins interact with receptors in our brain to reduce our perception of pain and increase our overall feeling of well-being. Laughter, which is often a common response to comedy, can also have physical benefits such as reducing stress hormones, increasing blood flow, and improving our immune system. In short, watching a comedy can have a positive impact on our mental and physical health by making us feel happier and more relaxed.

HOLLYWOOD COMEDY MOVIE

If you're looking for a Hollywood comedy movie that can help boost your mental health, I would highly recommend "Groundhog Day". This 1993 classic stars Bill Murray as Phil Connors, a weatherman who finds himself stuck in a time loop, living the same day over and over again. As he continues to re-live this day, Phil begins to re-examine his life and priorities, ultimately learning to appreciate the little things and finding joy in the present moment.

Not only is "Groundhog Day" hilarious and entertaining, it also offers a valuable lesson about the power of mindfulness and living in the moment. By the end of the film, you'll likely find yourself feeling more positive and optimistic about life. So if you're in need of a mental health boost, give "Groundhog Day" a watch!

list of some popular Hollywood comedy movies spanning different decades:

- **"Some Like It Hot" (1959)**
- **"Airplane!" (1980)**
- **"Ghostbusters" (1984)**
- **"Ferris Bueller's Day Off" (1986)**
- **"Groundhog Day" (1993)**
- **"Dumb and Dumber" (1994)**
- **"The Mask" (1994)**
- **"Clueless" (1995)**
- **"Happy Gilmore" (1996)**

- **"There's Something About Mary" (1998)**
- **"Office Space" (1999)**
- **"Meet the Parents" (2000)**
- **"Superbad" (2007)**
- **"The Hangover" (2009)**
- **"Bridesmaids" (2011)**
- **"21 Jump Street" (2012)**
- **"The Grand Budapest Hotel" (2014)**
- **"Deadpool" (2016)**
- **"Thor: Ragnarok" (2017)**
- **"Jojo Rabbit" (2019)**

This is by no means an exhaustive list, and there are many more fantastic comedy films out there. Comedy is a diverse genre, and these movies range from classic slapstick to witty and satirical humor.

CHAPTER 17, SPEND TIME WITH FAMILY

Research has shown that having strong relationships is a key component of happiness. Studies have consistently found that people who have close, supportive relationships with family, friends, and romantic partners are happier and healthier than those who do not.

One reason for this is that relationships provide a sense of belonging, which is a fundamental human need. Being part of a community and having people who care about us can help us feel more secure and fulfilled.

Relationships can provide emotional support during difficult times, which can help us cope with stress and adversity. Having someone to talk to, share our feelings with, and offer us encouragement can make a big difference in our mental health and overall well-being.

Research has found that the quality of our relationships is more important than the quantity. Close, intimate relationships with a few people tend to be more fulfilling and beneficial than having many acquaintances but no deep connections.

FAMILY IS THE FOUNDATION

"There is no doubt that it is around the family and the home that all the greatest virtues, the most dominating virtues of human, are created, strengthened, and maintained." This quote by Winston

Churchill perfectly encapsulates the significance of family. Our family is the foundation that shapes our character, morals, and values. They offer us unconditional love, support, and guidance throughout our lives.

Family is where we learn to communicate and develop social skills, and where we form lifelong bonds that provide us with comfort and security. It is through our family that we learn about empathy, compassion, forgiveness, and other fundamental qualities that make us better human beings. No matter how successful or accomplished we become, it is our family that remains a constant source of strength and inspiration.

In today's fast-paced world, where we are often distracted by technology and social media, it is more important than ever to prioritize family time. By spending quality time with our loved ones, we create lasting memories that we cherish for years to come. So, let us cherish our families and hold them close to our hearts, for they are the ones who truly make our lives worth living.

CREATIVE WAY WE CAN SPEND TIME WITH FAMILY

Spending time with family is a great way to strengthen relationships, create memories, and have fun. There are countless ways to spend time with your family, and here are just a few ideas:

1. Have a family game night: Gather around the table and play board games, card games, or video games together. This is a fun way

to spend time together while also stimulating your minds.

2. Go on a hike or nature walk: Get some fresh air and exercise while enjoying the beauty of nature. This is a great way to bond with your family and create lasting memories.

3. Cook or bake together: Choose a recipe and work together to create a delicious meal or dessert. This is a great way to teach kids about cooking while also spending quality time together.

4. Have a movie night: Pick a family-friendly movie and snuggle up on the couch with some popcorn. This is a relaxing and enjoyable way to spend time together.

5. Volunteer together: Give back to your community by volunteering at a local charity or organization. This is a great way to teach your kids about the importance of helping others while also spending time together.

No matter how you choose to spend time with your family, the most important thing is that you are together and enjoying each other's company.

Overall, it seems that building and maintaining strong relationships is an important factor in achieving happiness and a fulfilling life.

Chapter 18, Appreciate Others

"The roots of all goodness lie in the soil of appreciation for goodness." - Dalai Lama

As social beings, humans have a natural desire to feel valued and appreciated. When we receive appreciation from others, it reinforces our positive behaviors and makes us feel good about ourselves. This positive feeling can lead to increased motivation, improved self-esteem, and a greater sense of happiness and fulfillment in our lives.

Receiving appreciation from others can help us build stronger relationships and connections with those around us. When we feel appreciated, we are more likely to reciprocate those positive feelings towards others, leading to a cycle of positivity and mutual support.

WHY PEOPLE LOVE APPRECIATION

People love appreciation because it satisfies our fundamental need for social connection and validation. It helps us feel good about ourselves, strengthens our relationships with others, and contributes to our overall sense of well-being and happiness.

Appreciation is the recognition and enjoyment of the value, significance, or beauty of something or someone. People love appreciation for various reasons:

- **Validation:** When someone appreciates us, it validates our efforts and accomplishments, making us feel acknowledged and recognized.

- **Positive Reinforcement:** Appreciation serves as positive reinforcement. When people receive positive feedback for their actions, they are more likely to continue those behaviors.

- **Emotional Well-being:** Expressing or receiving appreciation can contribute to emotional well-being. It fosters positive emotions, such as happiness, gratitude, and satisfaction.

- **Building Relationships** Appreciation is a fundamental aspect of building and maintaining positive relationships. It strengthens the bond between individuals, whether in personal or professional settings.

- **Motivation:** Feeling appreciated can be a powerful motivator. It encourages individuals to put in extra effort and strive for excellence in their endeavors.

- **Cultural and Social Norms:** In many cultures, expressing appreciation is considered a polite and positive behavior. It aligns with social norms and contributes to a harmonious social environment.

- **Enhancing Self-Esteem:** Receiving appreciation can boost self-esteem and confidence, as it confirms that one's contributions are valued.

It's important to note that the expression of appreciation can take various forms, including verbal praise, written notes, acts of kindness, or simply showing gratitude. In interpersonal relationships, expressing appreciation contributes to a positive and supportive atmosphere, fostering mutual understanding and goodwill.

HOW TO APPRECIATE SOMEONE?

Appreciating someone is an important aspect of building and maintaining strong relationships. When you show appreciation to someone, you acknowledge their efforts and let them know that you value them. Here are some ways to appreciate someone:

1. Express gratitude: Say "thank you" and let the person know specifically what you are thankful for. Be sincere and specific in your appreciation.

2. Give compliments: Compliment the person on their strengths, skills, or qualities that you admire. This will make them feel valued and respected.

3. Show interest: Ask the person about their interests, hobbies, or passions. Show genuine interest in what they have to say and engage in conversation with them.

4. Spend time together: Make time to spend with the person and do

something that they enjoy. This shows that you care about their well-being and happiness.

5. Surprise them: Surprise the person with a thoughtful gesture such as a small gift or a kind note. This will make them feel appreciated and loved.

Remember, showing appreciation to someone doesn't have to be complicated or expensive. A simple gesture can go a long way in making someone feel valued and appreciated.

POWERFUL TOOL

Appreciation is a powerful tool that can be used to strengthen any relationship, whether it be personal or professional. There are many people and things that we can appreciate in our lives.

In personal relationships, we can show appreciation to our friends, family, partners, and even ourselves. We can appreciate the little things that they do for us, such as cooking a meal, listening to us, or simply being there for us when we need them. We can also appreciate the qualities that make them unique and special, such as their sense of humor, kindness, or intelligence. By expressing our appreciation, we can strengthen our relationships and make those around us feel valued and loved.

In a professional setting, we can show appreciation to our colleagues, employees, and bosses. We can appreciate the hard work that they put in, the skills that they bring to the table, and the contributions that they make to the success of the team or company.

This can be done through verbal recognition, written thank-you notes, monetary rewards, or other forms of acknowledgement. By showing appreciation, we can foster a positive work environment and increase motivation and productivity.

Overall, appreciation is a powerful tool that can be used to strengthen relationships, boost morale, and create a positive atmosphere. It is important to take the time to appreciate the people and things in our lives that make a difference, as this can have a profound impact on our happiness and well-being.

A hobby is an activity that a person engages in during their leisure time for pleasure or relaxation. Hobbies can vary widely and include things like reading, painting, playing sports, cooking, collecting items, and many others. People often pursue hobbies to relieve stress, learn new skills, express creativity, or simply enjoy themselves. Hobbies can be pursued alone or with others and can be a great way to meet new people who share similar interests. Whether you have a long-standing hobby or are looking to explore new ones, there is no shortage of options to choose from.

Engaging in hobbies is an important way for humans to improve their quality of life. Hobbies provide an opportunity to pursue interests outside of work or other obligations, and to have fun while doing so. Hobbies can help reduce stress and anxiety, improve mental health, and provide a sense of accomplishment and satisfaction.

Additionally, hobbies can be a way to connect with others who share similar interests, leading to new friendships and social connections. Overall, hobbies can be an important component of a well-rounded and fulfilling life, helping to promote both physical and mental well-being.

INTERESTING HOBBIES

There are countless hobbies that people can adopt to bring joy and fulfillment into their lives. Here is a list of some popular hobbies that you may find interesting:

1. Reading: Whether it's fiction, non-fiction, or poetry, reading is a great way to relax, learn, and escape into another world.

2. Gardening: Gardening can be a therapeutic activity that allows you to connect with nature, get some fresh air, and grow your own food.

3. Painting or drawing: Artistic expression can be a great way to relieve stress, boost creativity, and create something beautiful.

4. Playing music: Whether it's an instrument or singing, making music can be an incredibly fulfilling hobby that can bring joy to yourself and others.

5. Photography: Capturing beautiful moments and scenes through a lens can be a fun and rewarding hobby.

6. Cooking or baking: Experimenting with different recipes and ingredients can be a creative way to explore new flavors and cuisines.

7. Writing: Whether it's journaling, creative writing, or blogging, writing can be a therapeutic way to express yourself and share your thoughts with others.

8. Hiking or camping: Exploring the great outdoors can be a wonderful way to get exercise, connect with nature, and escape the stresses of daily life.

9. Collecting: Whether it's stamps, coins, or antiques, collecting can

be an interesting and engaging hobby that allows you to learn about history and culture.

10. Volunteering: Giving your time and energy to a cause you care about can be a rewarding way to make a difference in your community and the world.

explain to spend time to cultivate hobby and mental health.

MENTAL HEALTH & HOBBY

Spending time cultivating a hobby can be a great way to improve your mental health. Engaging in an activity that you enjoy and find fulfilling can provide you with a sense of purpose and accomplishment, which can boost your mood and self-esteem. Hobbies can also help you manage stress by providing a healthy outlet for negative emotions and allowing you to take a break from the pressures of daily life.

In addition to the immediate benefits of participating in a hobby, cultivating a hobby can also help you develop important life skills that can contribute to your overall mental health. For example, hobbies that involve physical activity, such as hiking or dancing, can improve your physical health as well as your mental health. Hobbies that involve creative expression, such as painting or writing, can help you develop your creativity and foster a sense of personal growth.

Ultimately, the key to using hobbies to improve your mental health is to find an activity that you enjoy and that provides you with a sense of fulfillment. Whether it's gardening, knitting, or playing music, spending time doing something you love can help you feel happier, healthier, and more connected to yourself and the world around you.

Journaling is the practice of regularly writing down your thoughts, feelings, and experiences in a notebook or journal. It can be done in a variety of ways, including free writing, prompts, and guided exercises. The purpose of journaling is to help you reflect on your life, gain insight into your thoughts and behaviors, and process your emotions. It can also be a helpful tool for setting goals, tracking progress, and improving your overall well-being. Journaling has been shown to have numerous benefits, including reducing stress and anxiety, improving mood, and boosting creativity. Whether you are looking to improve your mental health or simply want to become more self-aware, journaling can be a powerful tool for personal growth.

WHY JOURNALING IS IMPORTANT

Journaling every day is an important practice for many reasons. First and foremost, it provides a space for you to process your thoughts and emotions. Writing down your feelings and experiences can help you gain clarity and perspective on what is happening in your life.

It can help you track your progress towards personal goals. By writing down your accomplishments and challenges, you can identify patterns and areas for growth. This can help you stay motivated and make positive changes in your life.

Journaling can also be a form of self-care. Taking time to reflect on your day and write down your thoughts can be a therapeutic and calming activity. It can help reduce stress and anxiety and improve overall mental health.

TYPES OF JOURNALING

Keeping a journal is a great way to record your thoughts, feelings, and experiences. It can help you reflect on your life, track your progress, and gain insight into your own mind. There are many different types of journals you can keep, each with its own unique purpose and benefits. Here are some of the most common types of journals:

1. Personal journal: This is the most common type of journal, where you can write about anything you

want. It's a great way to express your thoughts and feelings, and to reflect on your life.

2. Travel journal: If you love to travel, this type of journal is for you. You can record your adventures, describe the places you visit, and capture your memories in words and pictures.

3. Gratitude journal: A gratitude journal is a powerful tool for cultivating a positive attitude. Each day, write down three things you're grateful for, no matter how small or insignificant they may seem.

4. Dream journal: If you're interested in exploring your dreams, keeping a dream journal is a great way to do it. Write down your dreams as soon as you wake

up, and try to interpret their meaning.

5. Fitness journal: If you're trying to get in shape, a fitness journal can help you track your progress. Record your workouts, your weight, and your measurements, and set goals for yourself.

6. Food journal: If you're trying to eat healthier, keeping a food journal can help you stay on track. Write down everything you eat and drink, and track your calories, nutrients, and portion sizes.

7. Reading journal: If you're an avid reader, a reading journal can help you keep track of the books you've read, and your thoughts and feelings about them.

SUCCESSFUL PEOPLE'S HABIT

Daily journaling is a practice that has been embraced by many successful people throughout history. One such person is Benjamin Franklin, who kept a daily journal for over 50 years. In his journal, he recorded his goals, thoughts, and reflections, and used it as a tool for personal growth and self-improvement.

Another successful person who practiced daily journaling is Oprah Winfrey. She has credited journaling as one of the keys to her success, saying that it helps her stay focused, reflect on her goals, and stay mindful of her progress.

In terms of how to practice daily journaling, there are many different approaches. Some people prefer to write in a physical journal with pen and paper, while others use digital tools like apps or online platforms. The key is to find a method that works for you and to make it a habit. Many people find it helpful to set aside a specific time each day for journaling, such as first thing in the morning or just before bed.

When it comes to what to write about in your journal, the possibilities are endless. Some people use their journal as a space to reflect on their emotions and experiences, while others use it to set goals and track their progress. Whatever approach you choose, the important thing is to be consistent and to use your journal as a tool for personal growth and self-reflection.

Overall, journaling every day can have numerous benefits for your emotional and mental well-being. It provides a space for self-reflection and can help you stay on track towards personal growth and development.

KEY BENEFITS OF DAILY JOURNALING

Journaling is an activity that has been proven to have numerous benefits for individuals who make a habit of it. Daily journaling, in particular, can provide a variety of advantages for your mental, emotional, and even physical health.

One of the key benefits of daily journaling is improved self-awareness. By taking time each day to reflect on your thoughts, feelings, and experiences, you can gain a deeper understanding of yourself and your emotions. This increased self-awareness can help you make more informed decisions and develop a stronger sense of self.

Another benefit of daily journaling is reduced stress and anxiety. Writing down your thoughts and feelings can help you process them and release any pent-up emotions. This can lead to a greater sense of calm and relaxation, which in turn can help reduce feelings of stress and anxiety.

Daily journaling can also be a great tool for setting and achieving goals. By writing down your goals and tracking your progress, you can stay motivated and focused on what you want to achieve. Additionally, journaling can help you identify any obstacles or challenges that may be preventing you from reaching your goals, allowing you to develop strategies to overcome them.

Overall, daily journaling can be a powerful tool for improving your mental and emotional well-being, as well as for achieving your personal and professional goals. Whether you prefer to write in a traditional notebook or use a digital journaling app, taking time each day to reflect on your thoughts and experiences can have a profound impact on your life.

TEMPLATE TO PRACTICE JOURNALING

Journaling is a powerful tool that can help us to process our thoughts and emotions, gain clarity, and track our personal growth. If you're looking for a template to help you get started, here's a simple one to try:

1. Date and time: Start by writing the date and time at the top of your journal entry. This will help you to track your progress and look back on your journey.

2. Gratitude: Begin your entry by listing three things that you're grateful for today. This could be anything from a good cup of coffee to a supportive friend or family member.

3. Reflection: Take a few minutes to reflect on your day or the events that have happened since your last entry. What emotions did you experience? What challenges did you face? What did you learn?

4. Goals: Write down three goals that you would like to achieve in the next week, month, or year. This could be anything from learning a new skill to improving your relationships.

5. Affirmations: End your entry by writing down an affirmation or positive statement about yourself. This could be something like "I am capable of achieving my goals" or "I am worthy of love and respect."

Remember, there's no right or wrong way to journal. The most important thing is to be honest with yourself and use your journal as a tool for growth and self-discovery.

CHAPTER 21, HELP OTHERS

Absolutely, helping others and engaging in acts of kindness can indeed contribute to feelings of happiness and well-being. Numerous studies and research in the field of positive psychology have explored the positive effects of altruism and kindness on an individual's mental and emotional state. Here are some reasons why helping others can bring happiness:

- **Release of "Feel-Good" Neurotransmitters:**
  - Acts of kindness have been linked to the release of neurotransmitters like dopamine and endorphins, commonly associated with

feelings of pleasure and happiness.

- **Reduction in Stress Levels:**
  - Helping others can have stress-reducing effects. Acts of kindness may trigger the release of oxytocin, a hormone that promotes bonding and reduces stress.

- **Enhanced Well-Being:**
  - Engaging in prosocial behavior, which includes acts of kindness and helping others, is associated with overall enhanced well-being and life satisfaction.

- **Positive Social Connections:**
  - Acts of kindness often lead to positive social

interactions. Building and maintaining social connections are crucial for happiness and a sense of belonging.

- **Sense of Purpose and Meaning:**
    - o Helping others can provide a sense of purpose and meaning in life. Contributing to the well-being of others can give individuals a broader perspective and a deeper sense of fulfillment.
- **Improved Mental Health:**
    - o Studies have suggested that volunteering and engaging in acts of kindness are linked to lower rates of depression

and anxiety. The act of giving can contribute to a positive mental state.

- **Positive Feedback Loop:**
  o Acts of kindness can create a positive feedback loop. When individuals experience the joy of helping others, it reinforces the likelihood that they will engage in more acts of kindness in the future.

- **Cultivation of Positive Traits:**
  o Engaging in kindness and compassion can help cultivate positive character traits such as empathy and altruism, which contribute

to an individual's overall sense of goodness.

- **Impact on Physical Health:**
  - Research suggests that helping others may have positive effects on physical health, including a potential boost to the immune system and cardiovascular health.

It's important to note that the intention behind the act of kindness plays a significant role. Genuine, selfless acts of kindness tend to have a more profound impact on well-being. Additionally, the nature of the act doesn't need to be grand; even small, everyday acts of kindness can contribute to positive emotions.

In summary, helping others is a powerful way to foster happiness, create positive connections, and contribute to a sense of purpose and fulfillment in life.

Mother Teresa is widely recognized for her acts of kindness and compassion towards the poor and sick. Throughout her life, she set countless examples of kindness that have inspired people all over the world. Her acts of kindness were not limited to any specific religion, caste, or creed and she devoted her entire life to serving humanity.

One of the most significant examples of Mother Teresa's kindness was her unwavering commitment to helping the poor and sick. She founded the Missionaries of Charity, which is an organization that provides aid and support to people in need all over the world. She also set up homes for the dying and destitute, and her efforts have helped countless people to live with dignity and respect.

Mother Teresa also believed in the power of small acts of kindness. She encouraged people to perform small acts of kindness as often as possible, as she believed that these acts could have a significant impact on the world. Some of the small acts of kindness that she encouraged included smiling at strangers, offering a helping hand, and being kind to those who are less fortunate.

In conclusion, Mother Teresa set numerous examples of kindness throughout her life. She dedicated her life to serving humanity and helping those in need, and her legacy continues to inspire people all over the world to this day. Through her work, she has shown that even the smallest acts of kindness can make a significant difference in the world.

KINDNESS & HAPPINESS

The notion that givers are often more achievers, successful, and happy is supported by research in the fields of positive psychology and social science. The philosophy of giving, often associated with altruism and generosity, can contribute to personal and professional success in several ways.

Firstly, givers tend to build strong and positive social networks. Acts of kindness, generosity, and genuine support create meaningful connections with others. These relationships, whether in personal or professional spheres, can lead to collaboration, opportunities, and a supportive environment. Success is often intertwined with the ability to build and maintain positive relationships, and givers excel in fostering connections that go beyond mere transactions.

Secondly, the act of giving can create a sense of purpose and fulfillment. Research has shown that individuals who engage in altruistic behavior and contribute to the well-being of others experience a heightened sense of meaning in their lives. This sense of purpose can be a powerful motivator, driving individuals to set and achieve meaningful goals. As a result, givers often find greater satisfaction and happiness in their personal and professional endeavors.

Moreover, the principle of reciprocity plays a role in the success of givers. When individuals are generous and supportive without expecting immediate returns, they often find that kindness begets kindness. Others are more inclined to reciprocate, creating a positive cycle of goodwill. In professional contexts, this can lead to increased collaboration, trust, and shared success.

It's essential to note that the effectiveness of giving lies in its authenticity. Genuine acts of kindness that stem from a true desire to contribute and make a positive impact are more likely to yield positive outcomes. When giving becomes a part of one's values and approach to life, it can lead to a more fulfilling and successful existence.

While being a giver can contribute to success and happiness, balance is key. It's important for individuals to establish healthy boundaries to prevent burnout and ensure that their giving is sustainable. However, when approached with authenticity and balance, the act of giving can be a powerful force for personal and collective well-being.

The idea that helping others leads to personal happiness is grounded in both psychological research and anecdotal evidence. When individuals engage in acts of kindness and altruism, it triggers a series of positive psychological and emotional responses that contribute to their overall well-being.

One significant aspect of this phenomenon lies in the release of neurotransmitters associated with happiness and reward. Acts of kindness, such as helping others, have been linked to the release of dopamine, a neurotransmitter associated with pleasure and positive reinforcement. This neurological response creates a sense of joy and satisfaction, forming the basis of the adage, "help others and be happy."

Furthermore, engaging in acts of kindness fosters a deeper sense of connection and social belonging. Human beings are inherently social creatures, and positive social interactions contribute significantly to mental and emotional well-being. When individuals help others, it strengthens social bonds, builds trust, and creates a sense of community. These positive social connections, whether in personal relationships or within the broader community, contribute to a lasting sense of happiness and fulfillment.

The concept of "help others and be happy" is also aligned with the principles of positive psychology, which emphasizes focusing on strengths, virtues, and factors that contribute to a fulfilling life. Acts of kindness are considered a pathway to enhancing one's sense of purpose and meaning, key components of a flourishing life. By extending a helping hand, individuals often find a deeper sense of purpose, contributing to an overall sense of happiness and life satisfaction.

Ultimately, the reciprocal nature of kindness reinforces the idea that helping others is not only beneficial to the recipient but also to the giver. Whether through small gestures or more significant acts of generosity, the act of helping others creates a positive feedback loop that enhances well-being, fosters a positive outlook on life, and contributes to enduring happiness.

This book offers the opportunity to identify your conscious and subconscious limiting beliefs and teach you scientific approach to eliminate them first and prepare you to use 9 Secrets of Subconscious Mind later, through many practical examples, techniques, stories, authentic breakthrough outcomes, and assignments.

★ *Your mind will be rewired while you read this book and you will be prepared to train your mind deliberately for day-to-day desired outcomes.*

✓ Do you want to help yourself?

✓ Do you think you deserve a better life?

If yes, then you will find amazing 9 secrets to manifest desired outcomes in your life in this book.

✓ **Many people try to heal their lives or try to make their lives better by Affirmations or by Meditation. Many people practice to write their desired goals, but don't get the results.** I was also on the same page. I practiced readymade affirmations and other modalities for many years to heal my life, I got results up to a certain extent but I was reactive and used to think and behave the same in adverse situation. My wisdom

246

didn't work for me in adverse situation or with no favorable people.

✓ Are you experiencing the same that I experienced earlier? In this case, not only read this book but also do all assignments given at the end of every chapter. **Consider this book is like a workbook** where you will learn new technique in every chapter, and you can immediately use all the tools and techniques through the assignment at the end of every chapter.

★ *Deliberate positive thoughts is our conscious choice and one must practice it consciously to train the subconscious mind every   moment.*
Be ready to manifest YOUR desired results through 9 secrets of subconscious mind.

Scan here to read.

Identify, Subconscious Limiting Beliefs to Alter Your Inner Critical thinking by Antidote Empowering Affirmations.

Rotten Fruits needs Root Treatment, Similarly, Core Limiting Beliefs need Conscious Efforts to Eliminate - Dipaali

1. Do you think you can do better in every area of your life but stuck somewhere?

2. Do you want to help yourself?

3. Are you utilizing your potential to the fullest in transforming yourself?

This book offers various opportunities to identify your Conscious and Subconscious Limiting Beliefs through questionnaires, and they allow you to tap unknown zone of your life where **Ecstasy** and **Abundance** are waiting for you.

You can closely work towards deep-rooted beliefs in every area of your life and can replace them with a collection of ***"Antidote Empowering Affirmations"***. They help you to improve your self-talk. You can reconstruct the new realities of your life with the help of useful techniques and tools which I have described in this book.

You have paid enough price in your life unknowingly, and now you have simple, easy, and profound methods in your hands in the form of this book. It helps you to bring a positive transformation into your life.

Weed out First & Seed it later.

It's impossible to implant new beliefs without identifying limited ones. Your mind will be conflicted by two different opinions on the same subject. On one side, you consciously choose to be wealthy, happy, healthy & spiritual, and on another side, your subconscious mind has already limiting beliefs in the same areas then your mind would be confused and not able to produce the desired outcomes in your life.

Most of the time people cannot identify their limiting beliefs and don't even able to address them. It is always important to identify our own Subconscious Limiting Beliefs first to implant *"New Antidote*

Empowering Beliefs" in our minds.

Part 1 & 2

You can use this book as an encyclopedia of Affirmations. You can find readymade dialogues to communicate to your subconscious mind easily and effectively. You will find the source of beliefs and behavioral science in part one, and you will have the opportunity to address your limiting beliefs in parts one and two of this book with the help of questionnaires.

Part 3

Of this book is the collection of ***"Antidote Empowering Affirmations"*** which you can practice to alter your inner critical self-talk.

This book offers powerful elimination processes of limiting beliefs and Antidote

Empowering Affirmations collection to eliminate the most common and dominant limiting beliefs of your life.

The entire book will prepare you to embed new empowering beliefs in your subconscious mind to manifest desire outcomes in your life. **Be ready to create an Affirmative World!**

Scan here to read

SECRET OF HAPPY LIFE

SECRET OF HAPPY LIFE

Conquer Your Inner World with Positive Self-talk. Master the Art of Forgiveness and Experience Joy. Fill Your Heart with Love and compassion.

- **Are you always sad, upset, fearful and angry with yourself and others?**
- **Do you need a reason to be happy?**
- **Is it always difficult for you to be happy forever?**

Happiness is the choice that one should make in life! You might have enough reasons to be sad and you always have the choice to find the bright side in every adverse situation to be happy.

Happiness comes to you when you,

- drop the traumatic past experience; and practice being in the present moment.
- embrace your strengths and weaknesses.
- practice altering your negative self-talk.
- learn to forgive others and have the courage to seek forgiveness.
- are grateful for everything you have in your life.

Your happiness doesn't depend on success in life, but your success definitely depends on your happy state of mind.

You will understand.

- the Law of KARMA.
- art and science to unloop KARMA to experience peace and joy in life.
- to identify your own inauthenticity and to help remove it.
- the power of positivity to alter life.
- why adverse people and situations come to life.

You will

- be happy in every situation.
- start loving yourself more.
- have the freedom to live life fully.
- be more grateful.
- have compassion in your heart for yourself and others.

You can

- celebrate every moment of life.
- experience joy in relationships.
- appreciate & accept others easily.
- be clearer in day-to-day life.
- stay healthy mentally and physically.

ABOUT Dipaali
I am the Life & iNNER WELLNESS Coach, and Author.

I am Mindfulness and meditation Coach, NLP Practitioner, Personal Mentor, and Corporate Trainer.

I offer Mental Well Being through the LAMP-N method. I am spiritually grounded and believe that "iNNER purity is more important than outer beauty."

MY JOURNEY OF TRANSFORMATION

No Person is a victim until he believes himself as one.

Being a victim

I considered myself a victim unknowingly since my childhood. I was shy, low-esteem, reactive, upset, and sometimes a rebel, because I believed that I was unloved, unsupported, unlucky and unwanted in my family.

We always talk about what we don't want, expecting that we will get what we want

I didn't know what I didn't know about my life

I didn't know what I wanted, and I used to complain about my life, my parents and my surroundings with others, expecting that I would get all pleasure, love and respect by complaining about unwanted people and situations in my life. Guess what happened to me!

I attracted more and more worst situations and people in my life as I didn't know the science that, "What we put attention on, Grows!"

Being upset, unhappy, resigned, reactive and rebellious, I had developed beliefs which were limiting me in every area of my life.

What's the truth? Beliefs create a human's character or human character creates beliefs?

The outcome of Limiting Beliefs

Being resigned and unhappy I attracted more toxic relationships and people in my life. The worse experiences went on, the stronger my beliefs got, and the more my beliefs became stronger, the more I became unhappy in life.

I was paying the cost in relationships, health, and career. I was always restless, anxious, fearful and angry.

I would love to help people but people didn't like to talk to me due to my reactive nature.

Though I was well-qualified, experienced and extremely hard working to gain profit in business, I was struggling as it was difficult for me to deal with the people in the business.

I was a nearly 80 kg bulky lady, neither fit physically nor mentally and emotionally.

Rotten Fruits need root treatment. Similarly, Core Limiting Beliefs need Conscious Efforts to Eliminate.

Being unaware, I went on to find solutions to my misery from astrology, Vastu science, worshipping in the temple, and by giving volunteer services to many religious organizations for many years.

I was working on the fruits rather than working on the roots, I didn't get results. I am not opposed to all these modalities, but working on fruits would never heal roots. These outer efforts didn't address the real root cause in my life.

My limiting beliefs designed my behaviors and character. They used to run my life and I was controlled by them.

In this breakdown time when there was no hope and happiness in life, one good habit of mine could help me transform my life, and that habit is "The habit of being a life-long learner."

My willingness to learn about life helped me identify my limiting beliefs and the root cause of misery.

Secret of Success Spend more Time and energy in Personal Development.

Many self-help books, personal development seminars, workshops, YouTube videos and courses have played an important role in my personal breakthrough results.

I bow down to all modalities and resources who have revealed the truth of life and poured wisdom in me.

I understood the secrets of life when I started implementing them in my life.

Let the past rest in peace! Create a Fantastic Future with a Positive Present Moment.

Sharing Wisdom:

1. I am responsible for all my current situations. I am taking the accountability of my life.

2. I love and accept myself

3. I love others unconditionally, as we are unique individuals and are connected with one divine energy, playing different roles on this earth realm in order to evolve.

4. I need to stay connected and nurture my inner child. I have started reparenting to my confused, upset and resigned inner child, who is always seeking love and security.

5. Forgiveness needs courage, and when you forgive others, you are ready to create a wonderful future in the present moment. I have forgiven everyone

whom I needed to forgive. I am free now.

6. Our body is a vehicle to experience all pleasure, and I am now more conscious about my lifestyle and food habits. I have been taking care of my body by practising yoga and eating sattvic food.

I choose to share my Love, Wisdom and Compassion with Humanity.

Decision

I paid a lot of costs for many years due to a lack of true wisdom in life. When I understood the importance of life coaching, self-help books, life-transforming YouTube videos and

Podcasts for personal development, and life-changing seminars, workshops and courses, I decided to educate others on the same.

I realized that everybody suffers in their life one way or another, and they don't know the correct solutions. They probably don't have the resources to alter their lives positively.

Being a Life and Inner Wellness Coach, I created my YouTube channel, launched podcasts, wrote self-help books and ran my online school for humanity to contribute to mental well-being in someone's life.

I believe: Inner purity is more important than outer beauty.

Achievements

I started my career as an educationalist in the year 2002 in Surat, Gujarat. During the 16 years of my journey, I have designed many vocational curricula in the field of computers and trained more than 1 lakh students with nearly 100% employment.

The government of India and the Government of Gujarat, UNO, South Gujarat Chamber of Commerce, Junior Chamber International and many more organizations have identified my efforts and intentions in the field of education through prestigious awards. I am grateful for all the love, respect, and recognition, I have received from society.

1. I have awarded the "Nari Gaurav" award on the occasion of "International Women's Day" by the SGCCI Ladies wing in 2016

2. I got the opportunity to have a very prestigious "KAMAL PATRA AWARD" for consistent professional growth and workmanship in business since 2002 by JCI in 2013.

3. I have been recognized with "The Saraswati Award" for contributing to the field of education and social work by "Achala Education Foundation Trust," Ahmedabad in the year 2013.

4. I had the privilege to be entitled the "ALL INDIA Achievers Foundation NEW DELHI" Award for her best performance in the field of education in the year 2010.

5. I am the first lady to be awarded the "Rajiv Gandhi International Award" for outstanding performance in Computer Education in 2006 at Gandhinagar by the Gujarat Governor.

Visit www.dipaali.life and book one 15 minutes complimentary one-on-one counseling for mental health.

Big Ask

Join me for an ongoing and upcoming life-changing workshop and help me to spread iNNER Purity in the outer world.
Kindly rate and write a review as an act of kindness. Your review matters to me and helps to humanity.

Google/Dipaali-life

https://g.page/dipaali-life?gm

Facebook/dipaali.life

Subscribe channel
YouTube/Dipaali

Follow me on

Instagram/dipaali.life
Connect me on
LinkedIn/dipaali.life